Public Administration
-Development, Scholars, and Theories-

Public Administration

-Development, Scholars, and Theories-

Tae Ryong Kim

Daeyoung Moonhwasa Publishing Company
Gyeonggi-do, Republic of Korea

Public Administration
-Development, Scholars, and Theories-

by Tae Ryong Kim

ISBN 978-89-7644-752-4
Published by Choon Hwan Lim
Daeyoung Moonhwasa Publishing Co.
Woosin Plaza 307 70, Juhwa-ro, Ilsanseo-gu, Goyang-si, Gyeonggi-do, Korea, 10387

TEL (031) 913-3062, (031) 914-3884~5
FAX (031) 913-3839
Hompage http://www.dymbook.co.kr
Published on 25 September, 2019

Price KR₩ 19,000

Preface

Having taught public administration as a professor for decades, I have always been told by students that it is difficult to understand what it is. Whenever I read introductory books on public administration published in Korea, I wonder how much first-year college students can understand these contents. Furthermore, the range of topics covered in introductory textbooks on public administration is so extensive that I cannot help but feel conflict as a professor when I think about whether students understood public administration at the end of the class.

Nevertheless, our situation is almost identical in all cases, and the core contents are almost composed of materials of American public administration textbooks. Besides, the majority of the theories created in the United States are delivered to students without any particular perspective, making it more difficult for students to understand.

If the study of public administration were made on our soil, it would be understandable even though the background of the contents or the environment of the time is almost understood, but it would be more challenging to understand because most of them have been formed based on the context and background of the United States. Besides, the number of international students studying in Korea is also increasing recently, and similar obstacles impede the understanding of public administration.

As a result, I could not help but agonize over how to improve understanding of public administration to students who are first exposed to public administration. I started from the idea of what I thought was the reason why students think that public administration is complicated. I have noticed that the students did not understand the background and development process of public administration correctly and that the scope of public administration was broad, so the students were too embarrassed to understand public administration.

Therefore, even if the scope of the public administration is broad among the two reasons why students have difficulty for studying public administration, I think that it would be somewhat helpful for students to study public administration if they understand the development background of the administration and the related theories correctly.

In the Korean context, where the history of modern civilization is short, it was inevitable that we could not but accept the contents of American public administration developed mainly in the United States. In this sense, it is a reality that students can not improve the understanding of public administration without the accurate knowledge of the development process of American public administration.

Then, there may be some counterarguments: Many introductory textbooks are dealing with the development and theories of American public administration in the United States, but why do I write American public administration?

There are, of course, many American-related public administration textbooks published in the United States. The problem is, however, that such books are too large in volume or unsystematic, making them less suitable as the introduction of public administration for Korean students or international students who have studied in Korea.

For example, to enhance students' understanding of public administration, the situation of the period of the development of the public administration, the view of the representative scholars who led the current location, and the theories created at that time must be linked organically. Only then can students understand the overall contents of administrative science systematically.

In this regard, I always felt sorry for the lack of suitable textbooks. Then, I started writing this book with all these aspects. Despite this purpose, it is challenging to describe all aspects of American public administration as essential knowledge for understanding public administration in a systematically and straightforwardly, including development processes, representative scholars' views, and administrative theories made at specific times.

Fortunately, I have already published the *Administrative Theory* that contains these contents more than a decade ago, and have now revised four times. However, the *Administrative Theory* is rather difficult for first-year college students and international students because of its large amount and confusing contents. Therefore, this book is not new, but it is a partial reorganization and correction of parts related to the American public administration which is the foundation of the public administration in the already published the *Administrative Theory*.

This book boldly omits elaborate footnotes or sources, and introduce the representative books that should be read in the reference section to help first-year college students and international students understand. Especially for international students who are not good at Korean language, Korean literature was boldly omitted. If students need more sources or references to the contents, they will be able to refer to the published *Administrative Theory*. In this regard, I would like to seek the reader's understanding.

Several people help in publishing even a little book. Above all, the beloved disciples who gave me this consciousness of a problem must be the best. Despite the somewhat complicated situation, family's interest in patience and encouragement has always been a boost. Among them, it was regrettable that I could not spend enough time with my beloved granddaughter, Na Hee, and Na Yun.

Finally, despite the questionable publishing circumstances, I am thankful to the president of Daeyoung Moonhwasa Publication Company, who publishes a little book and to the editorial department who has made efforts to correct the work.

Tae Ryong Kim
Seoul, Korea
Fall, 2019

Contents

Introduction

■ Cameral Science As a Foundation for Understanding the Birth of American Public Administration

As seen in the development of human history, humans have brought considerable attention to politics and government. However, just because various studies and practices have been carried out on the public sector, sporadically scattered ideas have not constituted an independent academic field. There have been many wise measures dealing with the public sector, but in practice, the administration has been treated as part of a political economy, military organization, or religious activities rather than being studied as an independent field.

Despite the historicity of research as a subject of public administration, until the 17th century in Europe, public administration could not be established as an independent discipline. The systematic study of public administration began to be established as an independent discipline and scholarship when the nation-state and the modern bureaucracy began to form.

In other words, the administration began to be formed as a branch and a discipline when the church and the state were separated, and the government had a universal authority over the society as a whole. Primarily, the bureaucratization has been proceeding due to the appearance of the nation-state, and the necessity of professional bureaucrats has been raised, and the administration of modern meaning has begun to appear.

The 17th century was the time when the term 'administration' began to appear in Europe when the domain of the monarch was divided into a public domain dealing with public affairs and a private domain dealing with the personal domain of the monarchy. It was also the time when the church and state were separated, and the government had power over social institutions within a specific territory. As a result, government activities have begun to emerge as areas of independent academic interest.

In Prussia, for example, a systematic study of administration has begun to prepare potential bureaucrats to perform government services. The study of public administration included all the fields of knowledge necessary for the rule of an absolute state. The model of the cameral science(Kammeralwissenschaft), which can be described as the administrative model of Prussia, has influenced many countries in Europe and the United States.

Thus, as a foundation for understanding the birth of American public administration, the meaning of cameral science is tremendous as a pioneer of public administration. In other words, Thomas Woodrow Wilson, the father of American public administration, thought that running the United States needed two axes. One is a democracy based on the civil society developed in Britain in political terms, and the other is the bureaucratic expertise through the cameral science developed in Prussia in terms of administration.

In this respect, it is significant to look at the meaning of the cameral science, so it helps to understand the characteristics of American public administration by looking at the characteristics of the cameral science that T. W. Wilson wanted to imitate.

In Europe, the birthplace of public administration was Prussian in the 18th century. The Kameralistik, or cameral science, which had begun to develop in Prussia, began as part of the administrative technique(Verwaltung skunstlehre), which educated and trained bureaucrats to achieve the goals of a nation oriented toward mercantilism and a centralized, unified nation.

Since then, Prussian public administration reached its peak in the 18th century. Prussian public administration at this time was called cameral science(Kameral) or police science(Polizeiwissenschaft). The cameral science was formed in close association with the formation of a modern state and encompassed all the contents of the reign of government required in an absolute monarchy.

This is why Prussia was able to establish a robust centralized regime after the Thirty Years' war in the 17th century. One was the cause of the collapse of the social status system and the feudal lordship system, and another reason was the existence of a trained standing army and organized administrative bureaucrats. In other words, in the process of establishing a robust centralized system, it was necessary to recruit soldiers and munitions together with the physical and financial demand for the operation of the state. This necessitated a comprehensive and efficient administration, which was cameral science.

Accordingly, in 1727, Friedrich Wilhelm I established an under-graduate course at Halle University and Frankfurt/Oder University to educate and train bureaucrats. Besides, he had established the cameral school in Lautern and Karl Schule in Stuttgart as a professional school for the education and training of bureaucrats. Cameral science was formed to support the economic and social revival of Prussia and thus the strengthening of the monarchy in the context of colonial occupation and foreign trade, followed by

Britain and France.

The contents of the cameral science covered all areas of political, economic, and social activity necessary to maintain absolute monarchy, and included areas such as agriculture, forestry, finance, economics, and police. The contents of the education covered in the cameral science mainly described the official institutions and functions of the government, with particular emphasis on the work of government officials and ethics of behavior.

Although the early cameral science formed in the 17th century encompassed various fields, the cameral science had a particularly strong financial character among them. Then, in the 18th century, with the maintenance of the police state system based on the Enlightenment absolutism, finance-oriented cameral science began to differentiate the police science into an independent discipline.

Johann Heinrich Gottlob von Justi, who laid the foundation for police studies, divided the purpose of the state into two parts. The first was the increase and maintenance of the national property, and the second was the effective use of the national property. J. H. G. von Justi has divided the primary purpose of the state as the promotion and maintenance of the national property, which is the responsibility of politics and police, and the second, the effective use of national property, as the field of finance.

He again separated politics and police science, which are responsible for the growth and maintenance of the national property. Among them, political science is a discipline dealing with the problem of internal and external security, which is the premise of maintaining national property. Moreover, police science is an academic study to maintain and enhance the national property as a whole based on the administrative system and realizing welfare through it.

In this sense, German police science became recognized as an administrative entity, which is an intrinsic national activity to realize the purpose or ideology of the state. As a result, German police science was recognized as a sort of public administration and later played a pivotal role in the formation of national administration and the completion of administrative science.

By the time police science was on the verge of spreading, the French Revolution had broken out; this had a decisive effect on the replacement of police science with administrative law again. In other words, when the French Revolution began to spread democratic ideas in Europe, the issue of civil rights, which had been neglected over the years, became a paramount concern.

This not only declines the influence of absolute monarchy but also has a profound effect on the academic legitimacy of police science developed under an absolute monarchy. As a result, administrative law replaced police science. The advent of administrative law has brought about the decline of the German public administration, the cameral science, the beginning of a full-fledged legal approach to administration, in the ideology of the rule of law, which has begun to prevail.

In the end, the cameral science is a product of different German mercantilism and absolutist Enlightenment ideology and was the prototype of the public administration including the contents of including economics, police science and finance for the property of the monarch and the management of the national treasury.

■ Genealogy of American Public Administration

Public administration has formed some theoretical genealogy, which is referred to by various names according to scholars. Examples include school, genealogy, paradigm, approach. However, theoretical genealogy differs according to development by each country and period, and even though it flourishes like a trend in a specific country, it is often replaced by another theoretical genealogy soon afterward.

The theoretical genealogies that have been formed in the field of public administration are generally similar to each other, but in some cases, they are classified by different criteria. Sometimes there are cases in which types that can be classified by different criteria are grouped. This is because scholars did not distinguish the theoretical genealogy of public administration by the same criteria, but also because of the theoretical genealogy that flourishes by country or period contain characteristics that can be classified by other criteria.

For this reason, unlike other countries, it is not easy to organize the development process of American administrative theory systematically. It is because more than 200 years had passed since the independence of the United States from the time when the fathers of the founding countries such as Alexander Hamilton, Thomas Jefferson, and James Madison were agonizing over the United States administration, and at least 100 years have passed since T. W. Wilson.

Also, there are many theories and methodology raised by administrative scholars at this time, and if we consider the theories, methodology, and the relationship borrowed from the adjacent academic field, it will be more challenging to understand the development process of administrative theory.

Therefore, the viewpoint of American administrative theory is diverse not only among American administrative scholars but also between Korean and Japanese administrative scholars. The difference between the theoretical lineages in the development of American administrative theory derives from the fact that each lineage is based on different criteria.

First, it is due to the differences in terms of epistemology and methodology. For example, approaches such as legal and institutional, behavioralism, postmodernism, or neo-institutionalism are distinguished by these criteria. Such differences are related to hypothetical theory, description, and explanatory meta-theory.

Second, it is due to an understanding of the political and economic context of administration, an emphasis on publicness, and a difference in the ideology involved. For example, the difference between politics-administration dichotomy and politics-administration monism, the relationship between public administration and private administration, and differences in the appropriate role scope of administration.

This is because it reflects differences in theoretical and empirical perspectives on the significance and status of administration in the context of relations between the state and civil society. It also reflects the relative importance of normative and instrumental theories related to values and prescriptions to be emphasized in administration.

Third, it is due to the differences in the range of subjects of the study of administration. For example, there are differences in genealogy depending on the case where the administrative research focuses on the internal management problem of the administrative organization, the case where the relationship between the administration and the political and economic environment is focused, and the case where the public policy is carried out by the administration.

The views of scholars about the development of American administrative theory are so diverse because it is based on different criteria. Since the criteria are different according to the object and focus as Robert Thomas Golembiewski states, the criteria for the characteristics are different as well as the difference in the time-division between the theoretical genealogy.

Although there are difficulties due to various reasons as the understanding of the development process of the American administrative theory is examined, there is a common point in the viewpoint of the development history of the administrative theory. In other words, some similarities are shared about the period, the subject and focus of the administration, and the values that have been pursued. Here, the development process of American public administration is divided into distinctive periods, and the views of representative scholars who led the period, and the dominant paradigm are introduced to enhance the understanding of readers.

Chapter I

The Infant Public Administration in the Beginning Period

1. The Story of the Infant Public Administration in the Beginning Period

During the centuries since the founding of the United States in 1789, the American political system was under the influence of the Jeffersonian-Jacksonian philosophy, which symbolizes liberal and democratic ideals. In other words, because the liberal political philosophy and ideas believed that government is best which governs least, it was very skeptical about the existence of the government itself. Because of Jeffersonianism, the American administration has become dominated by amateurism and public circulation.

However, the whole society was in crisis due to the capitalist malady caused by rapid industrialization and urbanization in the late 19th century. While the city was a place where immigrants formed a slum, it provided a cheaper labor force. On the other side, the gap between the rich and the poor grew as labor exploitation became more severe due to juvenile labor and long working hours.

More serious was the breakdown of democratic politics that had supported the United States since its founding. Grassroots democracy has long been a myth, as a new system that was settled in New England. An organized political mechanism centering around the city has blocked ordinary citizens to participate in politics and has created a crisis in the whole democracy.

On top of that, the harm has become very serious as President

Andrew Jackson's spoils system, which was carried out in the 1820s following the ideology of popular democracy and ordinary people's administration, degenerated into the practice of buying and selling government posts with the money. Due to the adoption of the spoils system, members of a political party who entered the government by exchanging their loyalty to a political party and public office. They were no different from the amateur in administration.

To make matters worse, as the 19th century began, the rapidly advancing industrialization and urbanization expanded and strengthened the role of the government, and the work of the government started to become more complex. As a result, the system of hiring public officials who do not have expertise in the administration to public office has become a significant source of administrative inefficiency.

Regardless of professional achievement, serious corruption in the process of occupying public office based on loyalty to the party was inevitable. The assassination of President James Abram Garfield in 1881 by a man who was frustrated with obtaining a public office was an example of the seriousness of the problem at that time. As a result, to overcome the overall crisis of the society in general, the intellectuals such as scholars, professional managers, lawyers, politicians centered on a kind of public reform movement called progressive movement.

As democracy has faced the crisis, progressive reformers have made the following arguments: First, it reformed the political system to guarantee more participation of ordinary citizens in the political aspect. Secondly, it advocated promoting efficiency-oriented work specialization, which was popular in the business management at that time from an administrative point of view. In other words, progressivists pursued strategies to accelerate democratization in the political arena to promote citizen participation while seeking to overcome the crisis of American democracy through a non-democratic way of specialization in the administrative sphere to substantially limit citizen participation.

As a result of the progressive movement, progressivists introduced direct democratic institutions such as referendum and recall into the political sphere. In the administrative field, they enacted the Pendleton Act in 1883. Thus, the political neutrality of the administration was declared, and a recruitment examination system was implemented to secure professionalism.

Meanwhile, it was Thomas Woodrow Wilson, who actively participated in the progressive reform movement in this background. The first direction of the reform movement, also called the economy and efficiency movement at the time, was to separate administration from politics so far as possible.

In line with the social climate at that time, T. W. Wilson believed that the United States would have to transplant and indigenize them into the United States by selecting the advantages of these systems by comparing the methodology of effective implementation of administrative work developed in Europe and the constitutionalism developed in the United Kingdom as a political system.

That is to say, T. W. Wilson thought that blooming British-style democratic political institutions through a German-style management method was an alternative for the United States to develop. The "Study of Administration," published by T. W. Wilson in 1887, included this content.

2. The Representative Scholars in the Beginning Period

To understand the characteristics of public administration of this period, the following is brief look arguments and contents of scholars representing this period.

2.1 Thomas Woodrow Wilson's Administrative Perspective

2.1.1 T. W. Wilson's Reform Movement

T. W. Wilson tried to find a new direction for political science. He emphasized that modern political science needed to pay more attention to how to manage the government, instead of engaging in the political maxim that the existing political science explored. The reason was that it was more challenging to operate a constitution than to establish it so that the time had come when political science had to find a new direction.

To this end, T. W. Wilson acknowledged that there was a subtle distinction between politics and administration, arguing that not only the personnel matters claimed by other reformers but also the organization and management issues should be addressed.

However, the delicate attempt to distinguish politics from the administration was a seemingly ordinary task, but at the time it was an essential political technique required in the course of the reform movement. This technique is because the argument that personnel issues should be based on appropriateness and performance rather than on partisan politics in the administrative sphere was an indispensable political tactic that the reform movement must possess to overcome the evils of partisan politics. Thus, this argument also meant that politics was not suitable for public services.

In other words, this meant that the administration had entered a new intellectual domain based on management science, on the premise that the administration would separate from traditional politics. So as a milestone for the American administration, T. W. Wilson pursued democratic administration. For example, public officials should be sensitive to public opinion, receive professional administrative education, comply with hierarchical disciplines. Besides, they should have responsibilities and dignity to meet the people's expectations.

2.1.2 T. W. Wilson's Political-Administrative Model

Until the nineteenth century, the study of government tasks mainly consisted of political philosophy, institution, or legislation. However, with the rapid change of the environment, new research fields have been demanded, and it has begun to emphasize the study of public administration focusing on the efficient operation of government tasks. In this regard, T. W. Wilson viewed politics as policy-making or enactment of an Act, while administration as a specific and systematic implementation of law or policy.

T. W. Wilson argued that the government should follow European-style administrative principles to support the system, even if the political system followed British constitutionalism. That is, the central tenets for the efficiency of government tasks were the same, also even if the form of government was different. Thus, T. W. Wilson defined that as the field of administration was a field of business, the administration was the management of the government tasks as businesslike.

However, at the time, T. W. Wilson's central concept was not recognized for its identity but was merely the first to assert the status of the administration, which had been subordinated to politics. He argued that it was necessary to adopt the advanced European administration developed under the absolute monarchy and develop it in harmony with the democratic political system of the United States. Therefore, T. W. Wilson is regarded as a scholar who first asserted politics-administration dichotomy, which means the separation of politics and administration.

T. W. Wilson attempted to distinguish the nature of administration from the field of politics by identifying it as a management domain. He defined administration as the field of management and business and the area of expertise and technology. The purpose of studying the administration is to explore what the government can do successfully and how it can do the work more efficiently with minimal cost.

T. W. Wilson provided a conceptual basis of administrative research by suggesting the need for separation of politics and administration and contributed to the foundation for the development of administrative science from politics to an academic discipline. However, he insisted that politics and administration should be separated, but failed to set the scope of the administration.

Consequently, he exposed the limitations of limiting the scope of administration to be a management tool of politics or law without definitively setting the range of the administration. Nevertheless, T. W. Wilson's claim to a separation of politics and administration does not necessarily imply that the administration should be disconnected from politics. His interest was in strengthening the executive power by putting power on the administrators.

From T. W. Wilson's point of view, many administrative scholars have presented administrative principles that are separate from politics. However, the scholars of those days can not be unconditionally construed as a politics-administration dichotomy. Mainly, they pointed out that the democratic government, which cannot effectively manage it, cannot be right.

In conclusion, T. W. Wilson's politics-administration dichotomy should be understood in the context of the liberal reform movement of the late 19th century. Rather than accepting the argument that politics and administration are irrelevant, the premise that the role of the administration is essential for democratic politics was developed through the discussion of the politics-administration dichotomy. Therefore, it would be fair to regard it as a paradox that the administration should be transformed into a de-political and technological figure to realize democratic politics.

2.2 Frank Johnson Goodnow's Politics-Administration Dichotomy

After T. W. Wilson, Frank Johnson Goodnow has attempted the thoughtful development of politics-administration dichotomy. He was the most central figure in the reform movement and the writer, and the first president of the American Political Science Association, in 1903. He made clear the difference between politics and administration in his book, *Politics, and Administration*, from the perspective of comparative administrative law in 1900.

One characteristic of F. J. Goodnow's achievements was that he pursued a legal approach in administrative research. As such, there was a tradition of studying administrative research in the legal sense at the time of American public administration. However, this approach has become invisible since then due to the dominance of the administrative research trend centering on administrative management theory.

His main concern was with how to set up a new political and administrative function to replace traditional matter, such as the separation of powers that deals with the allocation of power among governments. He tried brilliantly, though classic, to differentiate between politics and administration. He tried to analyze the differences between politics and administration through the concept of the expression of the will of the state and the execution of that will. Namely, he divided politics into expressing the intention of the country and implementing the policy, and administration into executing it.

F. J. Goodnow believed that excessive political party intervention in administration hindered the effective implementation of the policy. That is why he systematized the theory of politics-administration dichotomy that the administration should not only separate from political strife but also the policy-making process. His argument was then a great help in setting the direction of the municipal reform movement.

2.3 Frederick Winslow Taylor's Scientific Management Theory

In the same era that T. W. Wilson emphasized the need for a science of management, Frederick Winslow Taylor, called the father of scientific management, was building a scientific management theory, another axis of the basic theory of public administration. F. W. Taylor's scientific management had a profound effect on American society as it spread from the late 19th century to the early 20th century as a scientific management movement.

F. W. Taylor's famous work was *Principles of Scientific Management*, published in 1911. He gained nationwide fame when the House of Representatives' Special Committee held 'a hearing on scientific management' in 1912. Thus, scientific management theory has had a profound influence on the administrative field for the next 60 years since the beginning of this century.

The key to scientific management starts with the assumption that there is the best way to achieve a given task. Thus, scientific management seeks ways to increase output through the fastest, most effective, and least fatigued production methods. At this point, the responsibility of scientific managers was to impose this procedure on all workplaces if the best way was found.

In this respect, the classical organizational theory has evolved from F. W. Taylor's concept of scientific management. If there is the best way to accomplish a given task using scientific management concept, there will also be the best way to achieve the work of a social organization.

Despite criticism of the management theory centering on F. W.

Taylor, not only at the same time but also later, the contribution to the development of the administrative theory is substantial. For example, it became the first to use scientific methods and opened the way for further organizational research. Moreover, the methodology is a more inductive and empirical as compared to administrative management or bureaucratic theory. Besides, it can be recognized as a bottom-up study in the direction of research.

2.4 William Franklin Willoughby's Universality of Administrative Theory

While T. W. Willson turned into a politician, William Franklin Willoughby was a scholar with Frank Johnson Goodnow at the beginning of administrative studies. In particular, as a member of the Taft Commission, he played an essential role in drafting the Budget and Accounting Act of 1921. He has written extensively on public administration issues, among others, whose main idea was that the administration has a universal aspect that applies to all government agencies.

He wrote a three-part textbook in public administration that covered both the administration, the judiciary, and the legislature. Books in public administration were all published by the Brookings Institution. The first was *Principles of Public Administration* published in 1927 and the second was *Principles of Judicial Administration* published in 1929, and the last book was *Principles of Legislative Organization and Administration* related to the legislative administration in published in 1936.

Despite such a masterpiece, W. F. Willoughby seemed to have

had a particular interest in budget reform in the beginning. In *The Movement Towards Budgetary Reform in the States*, published in 1918, he contributed significantly to the creation of a contemporary budget system, albeit at the state level.

In this book, W. F. Willoughby argued that budget reform should include three characteristics. First, how can we develop and provide public control through the budget? Second, how can the budget strengthen the cooperation between the legislature and the administration? Thirdly, it was about how the budget could ensure management efficiency.

As we have seen, the theory of politics-administration dichotomy centered on T. W. Wilson, F. J. Goodnow, and W. F. Willoughby attempted to eliminate inefficiency, waste, and corruption in the administration by escaping administration from the pollution of party politics. Thus, the theory of politics-administration dichotomy became the theoretical cornerstone for the realization of a good government, and the foundation for establishing administration as an independent discipline. The theory of politics-administration dichotomy also provided the basic theory necessary for the development of the modern civil service system and the bureaucratic system.

However, despite its contribution, politics–administration dichotomy led to the loss of the consciousness of what it was to be a public administration. In particular, it is hard to avoid criticism in that it has resulted in the reduction and limitation of the essence of administration by focusing on the organization and management issues while losing interest in various purposes of the state in the development of public administration.

Despite various criticisms directed at the founders of early public administration such as T. W. Wilson, F. J. Goodnow, F. W. Taylor, and W. F. Willoughby, they have contributed to defining essential themes so that public administration can become a permanent research field.

The representative administrative theory that emerged in the beginning period of public administration is management theory. The background, characteristics, and contents of the theory that led to the formation of management theory are as follows.

3. The Representative Theory in the Beginning Period

3.1 Management Theory

By the time T. W. Wilson advocated the need for a science of management in 1887 as an alternative to improving the efficiency of administration, the American economic environment was also emphasizing efficiency in the wave of rapid industrialization.

As the market grew and mass production became possible in the wake of the Civil War of the 1860s, American companies began to expand rapidly. In the 1880s, the factory system was in full swing. However, the factory system based on mass production introduced a new production method called division of labor, which led to workers being subordinated to machines. As a result, the systematic protest of workers who oppose the new wage system and management methods has occurred frequently.

In the face of the crisis, the American economic environment needed to dispel concerns over workers' unemployment and low pay due to mechanization and division of labor and to ensure workers and mechanization that they were complementary rather than confrontational. So in 1880, the American Society of Mechanical Engineering was established to solve this problem. The efficiency movement took place around this association, and this movement was developed into management science.

The efficiency movement is not achieved only by the rationalization of the production method but becomes possible when it is associated with the efficient management of the production method. In this way, the efficiency movement has been fruitful with the development of scientific management, and F. W. Taylor's scientific management theory was at the center. F. W. Taylor's scientific management theory gained social acceptance, which was called the scientific management movement in the American social atmosphere at the time of its emphasis on efficiency.

Since then, scientific management has had a profound effect on the administrative work of the time, while occupying the position of social ideology or social philosophy, not merely of management, but in pursuit of efficiency in administration. In short, F. W. Taylor's scientific management theory was to pursue efforts for optimal management at the factory or operational level, namely the rationalization of production methods. Therefore, scientific management was a kind of micro approach.

On the other hand, after W. F. Willoughby published the *Principle of Administration* in 1927, a series of developing knowledge systems began to present administrative or organizational principles that could be applied at a more systematic level. These administrative principles and organizational principles have developed many concepts from a macro perspective, unlike a microscopic view that scientific management has emphasized. James Gardner March and Herbert Alexander Simon called these concepts, which were carried out from a macro perspective, as administrative management theory.

In conclusion, if the scientific management theory was a theory focused on improving the productivity of the workers at the level of the workplace, the administrative management theory was to maximize efficiency by integrating organizational members at the upper level of the organization. Therefore, two approaches are collectively referred to as management theory in that they pursue the attribute of efficiency in common, except for differences according to the level of application.

Meanwhile, scientific management theory and administrative management theory have developed with the time difference, and there is a difference in the level of analysis so that they can be separate theories. However, except for these differences, the two approaches have a common point of management theory in that they sought to pursue efficiency.

Despite some differences between the scientific management theory and the administrative management theory, both approaches have set the primary purpose of improving the efficiency of the organization from a closed-system perspective, and have a common point in that they emphasize the formal structure and process to improve efficiency. Therefore, it is not unreasonable to group the two theories into the category of management theory.

3.1.1 The Scientific Management Theory

1) The Background of Theory

The scientific management theory centered on F. W. Taylor was a product of the economic situation of the 1900s when the population rapidly expanded, and industrialization was promoted. At that time, the managers of the factory had to hire and manage the workers who had not experienced.

In this context, scientific management has focused on increasing productivity by making more efficient use of the workforce. To this end, the scientific management theory has focused on segmenting the division of labor as a way to increase the production rate. In other words, the main goal was to complete the work efficiently and economically through the division of labor.

F. W. Taylor and his successors also emphasized planning. For example, F. W. Taylor focused on rigorously examining the physical conditions of the workforce, especially the physical abilities of the worker. F. W. Taylor wanted to select a worker who was deemed suitable for a particular task, to work at various speeds and tried to find the optimum working speed and break time. In other words, F. W. Taylor attempted to find the best way scientifically through a study of time and motion.

The scientific method thus began with the underlying assumption that human motivation theory and interests between workers and organizations are common to each other. F. W. Taylor thought that because human beings have a desire to make money in essence, it is necessary to link the wages to productivity to increase efficiency. F. W. Taylor believed that a rational worker would try to maximize his income and that the physical ability of the worker would determine his maximum profit. In the case of managers, if the production rate increases, the total wage will be lowered and the profit will increase, which will help the manager because it will be the basis for raising the salaries of the workers again.

After all, Taylorism centered on F. W. Taylor and his successors, was the theory shaped by the influence of Protestantism ethics, rationalism in economic philosophy, and engineering thinking. In other ways, the scientific management school started based on respecting the virtues of hard work, economic rationality, and individualistic values.

2) The Purpose of Scientific Management

F. W. Taylor's work on scientific management, *The Principles of Scientific Management*, was published in 1911, and the first sentence of this book begins with: "The primary purpose of management is to create the greatest prosperity of employees, along with the greatest prosperity of labor."

The purpose of this book was as follows. It began with the assumption that if there were the best way to get away from the traditional management style of management and operation of the organization and achieve the given task, then there would also be the best way to make the organization's work. He sought to maximize human and mechanical efficiency by finding scientific principles through time and motion studies.

Accordingly, the four principles of scientific management that advocated by F. W. Taylor are a kind of guideline for managers, as follows:

First, in the process of measuring and managing workers' work factors, it is necessary to replace them in a more systematic and scientific method by avoiding the old rule of thumb management. Second, workers should be selected scientifically during work, and training and educating chosen workers should develop the potential. Third, it is most important to get workers' cooperation to apply scientific principles. Fourth, it is necessary to distribute work and responsibility evenly between manager and worker to minimize conflicts in management.

The key techniques presented in scientific management include time and motion study, standardization of tools, task management, and differential piece-rate systems.

3) The Contents of Scientific Management Theory

F. W. Taylor's scientific management theory has argued that management should be based on the following principles concerning work and the workplace, as well as obligations that must be obeyed by managers. In other words, the prescriptions and principles of scientific management are as follows:

First, time and motion study should be done to find only one best way to perform a task. At this time, the best approach means an alternative that maximizes the daily production rate. Second, it is necessary to provide financial benefits so that workers can perform their duties in the best way possible. It is desirable to introduce a differential piece-rate system based on productivity as a way of providing financial benefits to workers. Third, there should be a small group of experts to assist in various situations surrounding the work of the workers. Fourth, the principle of preventing modifying the standard production rate arbitrarily should be established.

F. W. Taylor's scientific management theory emphasized that the mental revolution must be made simultaneously for these prescriptions and principles to be successful. To sum, the essence of scientific management was viewed as a mental revolution, an excellent way of thinking. F. W. Taylor argued that two modes of cultivating labor-manager cooperation and scientific thinking could lead to a spiritual revolution.

3.1.2 The Administrative Management Theory

1) The Theoretical Characteristics

Scientific management is a micro approach that focuses on workers at the workplace level in terms of analytical level. Therefore, to increase the overall efficiency of the organization, there was a limit to the rationalization of the whole organization by improving the level of the workplace, such as scientific management theory. This is because not only is the rationalization of the process of linking the organization's purpose to the production site, but also the productivity of the manager is equally essential. In this regard, administrative management theory is the first to raise management problems. Therefore, administrative management theory can be regarded as a complementary relationship with scientific management theory.

The administrative management theory then adopted efficiency as a fundamental value and focused on studying the structural relationship of organizational units, types of management functions, management process, principles related to the division of work and organization. The so-called principles developed in administrative management theory have been usually about the differentiation(a division of work) and integration(coordination) of organizational activities.

Administrative management theory believed that efficiency could be enhanced by a rational division of labor(specialization), collectivization of a division of work(departmentalization), and coordination. Specially, it viewed the division of work and coordination as a critical element of organizational management, and focused on developing the principle of division of work, the principle of unity of command, the principle of span of control, the principle of coordination, the principle of scalar chain, the principle of departmentalization, etc.

Henri Fayol, Mary Parker Follett, Luther Gulick, Lyndall Fownes Urwick, James David Mooney, and Alan Campbell Reiley, who proposed the principles in terms of administrative management theory.

2) The Contents of Administrative Management Theory

The main contents of the administrative management theory are as follows, focusing on the POSDCoRB of L. Gulick and L. F. Urwick.

Anglo-American academic circles introduced H. Fayol's management principles in the 1930s, which had a profound impact on subsequent administrative management theorists. L. Gulick and L. F. Urwick, in their *Papers on the Science of Administration*, published in 1937, pointed out that H. Fayol's influence on their management principles was significant. Based on his experience in corporate management and government operations during the 1920s and 1930s, they sought to shed light on the definitions and principles of management, which was published in 1937.

The papers published in the *Papers on the Science of Administration* edited by L. Gulick and L. F. Urwick were mostly about the principles and standards for organizational management. For example, the main content is about the function of a manager, the principle and standard of departmentalization, the principle of division of work and specialization, the principle of unity of command, the principle of span of control, and the principle of coordination, which is not much different from what H. Fayol argues.

In this book, they listed the functions that top managers should perform: planning, organizing, staffing, directing, coordinating, reporting, and budgeting. These functions have since been referred to as POSDCoRB along with the initials, which not only indicate the role of the manager but also refer to the scope and subject of the later study of public administration.

However, they paid great attention to the criteria for the formation of a department and departmentalization, that is, the division of work within the organization in this book. They presented the following four factors as the criteria required in the process of decentralization, from the point of view that division of work is the basis of organization and the reason for the existence of the organization.

They emphasized that division of work should be done according to the purpose and function necessary for the division of labor, the process or procedure to be used, the things and person to be treated, and the place or area where the activity is performed.

3.1.3 The Relevance of Management Theory

1) The Critique of Management Theory

Criticism of management theory can be divided into criticism of scientific management theory and criticism on administrative management theory. A brief review of the criticism is as follows:

First, despite many contributions, scientific management theory has had problems in managing organizational members based on mechanical principles rather than humans. By treating human beings with irrational and emotional characteristics as merely mechanical, rational, and inhuman tools, scientific management theory was faced with criticism that it would somewhat reduce voluntary productivity.

In particular, the expansion of the division of work by the adoption of scientific management theory increases in the cost of coordination and control of the organization, and more importantly, a reduction in social interaction among employees, resulting in more losses than gains from the expansion of the division of work.

As a result, both labor and management criticized scientific management theory. Employers criticized the authority of entrepreneurial as being replaced by the knowledge of engineers, and workers criticized it as an inhumane theory of seeing people as accessories of machines.

Second, the contribution of administrative management theory is to explore and establish the universal principles of the organization above all. However, similar to the scientific management theory, administrative management theory has been criticized much about propositions and principles. In other words, the concept of principles is not universal, and the idea of principles is both ambiguous and contradictory.

2) The Applicability of Management Theory

The criticism of scientific management theory and administrative management theory is imposed by the lack of understanding of human nature and the unproven abstract principles as shown above. Scientific management theory and administrative management theory indeed have many limitations, but on the other hand, these theories have a significant impact on administration and organizational management.

The effect of administrative theory, especially on the development of organizational theory, is not only significant, but also the effect of them on the practical side cannot be denied. For example, scientific management theory has provided concrete scientific methods to increase productivity. It is disproving that time management or second management is widespread in the management field today.

In particular, in the case of organization diagnoses conducted to increase productivity in the organization, job analysis is performed. This is also the main content of F. W. Taylor's scientific management theory. However, more importantly, F. W. Taylor's real intention was not to alienate workers through a division of work, but rather to seek ways for users and managers truly coexist by improving productivity through division of work. Thus, if F. W. Taylor's true intentions are highlighted, the pure function that scientific management has sought to pursue is bound to continue in the management field.

Finally, many scholars, including H. A. Simon, has criticized the concept of management and principles that administrative management theorists have argued for being merely an unproven proverb, but the theories they advocated were also concepts built through experience in the management field. Thus, although the limits of the principles are partially present, the values of these principles have not disappeared. Several principles are still applied today. In this respect, administrative management theory can be regarded as preserving its value as a theory despite its problems.

Chapter II

The Orthodox Public Administration in the Formative Years

1. The Story of the Orthodox Public Administration in the Formative Years

During this period, from 1918 to 1941, when World War I ended, the American administration has undergone tremendous changes. As the war ended, the American government returned to pre-war form, but the influence of the government on American life was not diminished. At this time, the United States began to shift from agricultural to urban industrialized countries, and this change in the environment has begun to demand much change in administration.

The change has created many new functions and programs in this process. In particular, the explosive urbanization of the 1920s and the Great Depression of the 1930s have further fueled the role of the federal government.

For example, by the 1920s, the highways had increased tenfold. Also, the city began to install a traffic management system with an explosive increase in traffic volume, and the state forced the driver's license test. Notably, the problems of parks, leisure, public works, public hygiene, and public safety have begun to emerge as an essential agenda due to the rapid increase in the population of the city. Because of these causes and activities, the administration developed rapidly in the 1920s.

As a result, the American public administration, which started from the practical political reform movement to overcome the illness of the spoils system and to build an efficient administration, was later established with its academic field combined with scientific management theory and classical organizational theory. Besides, as a new concept of value-oriented toward the realization of economy and efficiency, the American public administration has become the orthodox public administration characterized by the management science that advocated efficiency-based management from the 1920s to the 1930s.

As Dwight Waldo pointed out, this period, which could be defined by the end of World War I and the rise of World War II, was a period of orthodoxy, and the public administration made rapid progress. The ideological trend of this period was considered to be the same meaning or at least harmonious with democracy and efficiency. It was also the period when government work could be divided into decision-making and executive areas, and public administration was regarded as a science with principles.

In this period, the administrative theory comes to the development of administrative management theory as classical organizational theory joins the administrative theory concentrated on the theory of politics-administration dichotomy. The administrative theory centered on administrative management has developed a series of research activities to streamline management activities belong to the area inherent in the administration and integrating and strengthening executive power.

Meanwhile, in the field of organizational theory in the formation and development of orthodox public administration, scientific management theory aiming at the scientification of work and organizational management theory aiming at the scientification of organization emerged.

The orthodox public administration as a management science has significantly contributed to maintaining the dominant self-identity in American public administration until it faced with criticism through the experiences of the Great Depression and the New Deal. In the end, it was the two paradigms of politics-administration dichotomy and the principle of administration that formed the foundation of orthodox public administration.

At the same time, the development and expansion of the city manager system are characteristic of the development process of administrative theory. Since the establishment of the City Manager's Association in 1914, the city manager system has rapidly spread across local governments. The expansion of the city manager system brought about the creation of the graduate school of public administration, which provided an opportunity for the development of administrative theory as well as the production of professional administrators.

In particular, with the establishment of the graduate school of public administration, the American Society for Public Administration was founded in 1939 as an academic community of administrative scholars. The following year, the publication of the Public Administration Review, the editor-in-chief of Leonard Dupee White, marked another milestone in the development of administrative theory. Also, the Brookings Institution was established in 1927.

2. The Representative Scholars in the Formative Years

The arguments and contents of scholars representing this period are as follows.

2.1 Max Weber's Bureaucracy Model

The first analysis of the bureaucracy that emerged as a dominant feature at this time began with the German sociologist Max Weber. The analysis of the bureaucracy published in 1922 was the most influential study that was the starting point of bureaucratic research.

M. Weber played an essential role in establishing the constitution of the Weimar Republic of Germany in 1920, just before his death. However, the experience M. Weber had gained in this process gave him considerable strength to realize that it was more challenging to run a constitution than to establish a constitution, which was the subject of T. W. Wilson's concern.

M. Weber's work on the bureaucracy was translated into English in 1946, but his influence was enormous. It is because M. Weber emphasized a new methodology for developing organizational studies. The new methodology, that is, the characteristics of the bureaucratic organization proposed by M. Weber, provided an essential reference for evaluating the positive and negative effects on the bureaucratic structure for orthodox administrative theorists and critics.

The theory of authority structure was the basis of M. Weber's bureaucracy theory. M. Weber contributes to presenting the ideal type of rational and legal bureaucracy based on rational-legal authority. At this time, ideal type refers to a kind of abstract framework.

M. Weber categorized the types of authority as charismatic, traditional, and rational-legal authority. Among them, the bureaucratic model based on rational-legal authority was considered the most suitable to describe the large-scale organization of modern society. For example, it is the bureaucracy that has elements and characteristics such as the rule of law, hierarchical structure, specialization, dedicated staff, payroll, a distinction between office and member's house, red tape.

The bureaucracy is rational because it is a means or a tool that consciously designed to achieve a specific goal, and it is legal because authority is exercised through a legal and procedural system. In other words, M. Weber presented the bureaucracy as a representation of rationality, when the leader of an organization with rational authority makes decisions, and subordinates automatically and promptly and faithfully obey the orders.

The most basic value standard in the bureaucracy model proposed by M. Weber was efficiency. M. Weber believed that bureaucracy is designed to define positions according to the jurisdictions and hierarchy, to assign professional staff in the positions, to set rules on types of activities, and to stimulate the performance of professional staff through remuneration and promotion. Accordingly, the bureaucracy could increase efficiency by ensuring accuracy, speed, clarity, uniformity, through the obedience of subordinates, reduction of friction, and reduction of human and physical costs in the performance of the mission.

M. Weber's bureaucracy model has since had a profound impact on administrative theory, and at the same time, he faced many criticisms due to the limitations of the bureaucratic inefficiency or pathology that M. Weber overlooked.

However, while criticism of M. Weber and the pathological phenomenon of bureaucracy must be overcome, but if people understand the circumstances and intentions of the times when Weber had to propose an ideal type of bureaucracy at this time, criticism of M. Weber should be considered a problem to be dealt with in another area.

M. Weber was a critic of bureaucracy in a sense rather than an advocate of bureaucracy. He supports this by predicting that the current trend of bureaucratization will one day be an inexorable force to overwhelm capitalism. He warned that in a bureaucratic society that would come in the future, humans would be forced to enslave, and he sought to find ways to effectively control the enormous bureaucracy, wondering how to keep individual freedom, creativity, and accountability in the process of bureaucratization.

Although M. Weber's bureaucracy model has pursued efficiency in this respect, it is difficult to classify it as T. W. Wilson's administrative principle or F. W. Taylor's scientific management theory.

2.2 F. W. Taylor Type and Anti-Taylorian Managerialism

Since the end of World War I, the concept of management has begun to spread in all areas, regardless of public or private sectors. Thus, scientific management or Taylorism began to form a dominant atmosphere in all areas of administration, and Leonard Dupee White, a representative scholar of this period. If T. W. Wilson, the father of public administration, developed the logic that administrative field should exist as a discipline and an area of professional specialty, L. D. White was the first scholar to set the precondition of public administration.

The *Introduction to the Study of Public Administration* published in 1926 was the first administrative textbook in this regard. In the preface, L. D. White described four critical assumptions that are fundamental to forming a foundation in the study of public administration:

First, the administration is a single process that can be equally studied at the federal, state, and local levels. Second, the basis of research lies not in the law but management. Third, the administration is still art. Nevertheless, the effort to convert to science is feasible and valuable. Fourth, the administration had existed and continues to exist at the heart of problems of the current government.

L. D. White emphasized the prescriptive approach of administration as such and recognized administration as the research area that should remain close to the actual society. In particular, L. D. White emphasized the management aspects of administration instead of being caught up in the controversy of politics-administration dichotomy. For example, L. D. White avoided debates on issues such as the extent to which the administration itself should participate in shaping the purpose of the state, or the exact nature of administrative activities.

Meanwhile, the challenge to the scientific approach was conducted by Elton Mayo and colleagues at the Hawthorne workshop near Chicago, from the late 1920s to early 1930s. The main content of the experiment over a decade or so was to validate the relationship between work environment and productivity with traditional scientific management theory.

However, the results of the experiments showed unexpected results. From today's point of view, the slightest thing brought a great wave back then. It was a fact that workers were more sensitive to the social pressures they received from colleagues than to the management by control, one of the traditional scientific management techniques.

Since then, the traditional scientific management theory faced a situation in which the social situation or the psychological aspect emphasized by the human relations school centered on Hawthorn cannot but be regarded as another significant source of productivity.

The traditional scientific approach was also attacked by Chester Irving Barnard, whose position has evolved into a comprehensive theory through *The Functions of the Executive*. He regarded the organization as a cooperative system and viewed it as a function of the manager to maintain a dynamic balance between the demands of an organization and the needs of workers.

C. I. Barnard emphasized that if managers are to perform their functions properly, managers must understand the attribute of an interdependent relationship between formal and informal organizations. Thus, C. I. Barnard emphasized the importance of informal organizations that traditional scientific approaches have neglected.

2.3 Carl Joachim Friedrich and Herman Finer's Administrative Responsibility

At this time of the formation of public administration, the development process of administrative theory did not remain solely in efficiency or productivity, which is a problem within the administration. In other words, the focus of administrative theory was not only on the administrative aspects of management such as organizational behavior and structure, budget and personnel, which are internal problems of administration but also on the external aspects of administration such as the concept of administrative responsibility.

Carl Joachim Friedrich and Herman Finer raised discussions on the external aspects of administration from the late 1930s to the early 1940s. There was a heated debate between the two over how to secure administrative responsibility. In this debate, C. J. Friedrich argued that it was most useful to secure administrative responsibility through internal controls such as professionalism, professional standards, or ethical charters. In 1939, when this debate was in full swing, the Presidential Secretariat was created following the Reorganization Act.

On the other hand, H. Finer was in a position that administrative responsibility must be maintained through legislative and public control. The external constraints and the balance through it were the only way to maintain bureaucrat's obedience. The reason why external control is so superior to internal control is that internal power can cause corruption, so internal control has to be limited. Therefore, external control for controlling bureaucrat's corruption and injustice is possible only through election or strict supervision by the legislature.

3. The Representative Theory in the Formative Years

The representative administrative theory that emerged in the formative period of public administration is bureaucracy theory. The background, characteristics, and contents of the theory that led to the formation of bureaucracy theory are as follows.

3.1 Bureaucracy Theory

The term 'bureaucracy' can be found in 1745 when Jean C. M. V. de Gournay first used it. According to Jean C. M. V. de Gournay, the word 'bureau,' which means desk and office, became a bureaucrat by attaching 'cracy,' a Greek suffix meaning rule. As a result, the bureaucracy began to be used to refer to the rule of bureaucrats.

The bureaucracy was a concept that reflected the rise of the national power in the 18th century and the emergence of the management group as an emerging force accompanying it. So the bureaucracy emerged as one of the forms of government, contrasting with the monarchy or aristocracy at the time. Therefore, the definition of bureaucracy that appeared in the dictionary published in European countries at that time was related to the meaning of force or power of government offices or management groups, similar to Jean C. M. V. de Gournay's view.

3.1.1 The Background of Bureaucracy Theory

It was in the early 19th century that the bureaucracy began to appear in political studies in earnest, although Germany was exposed to the term bureaucracy through newspaper reports on the French Revolution. It was Johan Görres who played a significant role in the dissemination of bureaucracy.

J. Görres considered the concept of bureaucracy as an administrative skill that could fill the gaps in the lack of trust between the ruler and the governed since it was based on principles such as discipline, promotion, dignity as a group, and centralization. Thus, he called the bureaucracy a civilian system similar to the standing army. He also saw that the bureaucracy would succeed in integrating the masses, as it would extend the principles of obedience from its organic organization to the subjects while defining human values as derived from status, not from themselves.

However, despite the conceptualization efforts of scholars such as J. Görres, the concept of bureaucracy that was used in Germany only highlighted negative images amid confusion. For example, in the nineteenth century, with the form of governance in Germany, it was also used to refer to administrative arrangements and inefficient governments.

If the concept of the bureaucracy had spread to Germany in the aftermath of the French Revolution, Britain introduced the concept of bureaucracy mainly through German literature. In the early days of Britain's introduction of bureaucracy, the position on the concept of bureaucracy is reflected in the view of John Stuart Mill.

J. S. Mill said bureaucracy does not exist in the United Kingdom, and bureaucracy is unnecessary because the United Kingdom firmly established democracy. J. S. Mill concluded bureaucracy as an enemy of freedom and democracy by claiming that bureaucracy monopolizes society's abilities and behaviors not only make political life incompetent but also that both the ruler and the governed become slaves to bureaucracy.

By the end of the nineteenth century, the issue of bureaucracy was coming to reality in the United Kingdom. The bureaucracy came to be a matter of reality due to the reform of the civil service system in the 1870s. As Stafford Northcote, the animateur of reform, reformed the civil service system, he thought that lifelong civil servants would dominate public affairs from 1884.

As a result, he warned of bureaucratic tyranny, saying that Congress would almost disappear. Thus, the United Kingdom regarded the bureaucracy as the cause of the crisis of parliamentary democracy.

3.1.2 The Contents and Characteristics of Bureaucracy Theory

1) The Concept of Bureaucracy

The concept of bureaucracy is not easy to define because of its diversity and instability. The concept of bureaucracy is defined differently, even in the same scholar—for example, even Max Weber defined the bureaucracy as an organization that in some cases had a significant set of structural features and functional styles, while in other cases, he defined the bureaucracy as a social organization that maximized management efficiency.

The concept of bureaucracy is so unstable because, as Martin Albrow pointed out, there is an entirely different concept of using the same name as bureaucracy. That is, in the modern context, scholars use the concept of bureaucracy in seven different cases. However, notwithstanding these various definitions of bureaucracy, one of the universal phenomena surrounding the concept of bureaucracy after M. Weber developed bureaucracy theory is that the concept of bureaucracy began to be approached from the standpoint of the characteristics of the organizational structure.

Therefore, we would like to follow the conceptual definition of bureaucracy based on M. Weber's perspective, among various conceptual perspectives surrounding bureaucracy. In other words, in M. Weber's view of bureaucracy, bureaucracy is a social organization with an array of structural characteristics and functional style that maximizes management efficiency.

2) The Proposition and Characteristics of Bureaucracy Theory

In discussing the characteristics of bureaucratic theory, the most important is the theory of authority structure, which is the core of M. Weber's bureaucracy theory. In other words, a discussion of the source of legitimacy on which authority is based is a cornerstone of the theory. The first thing to mention is dealing with the characteristics of the bureaucratic theory is the discussion on legitimacy as the basis of authority. M. Weber's authority structure in this regard is as follows.

According to M. Weber, when an organization performs its tasks, an organization relies on three types of authority. First, it is charismatic authority. The charismatic authority is the case in which the command from him is justified because of the belief in the extra-ordinary qualities possessed by a particular person. Second, it is traditional authority. The traditional authority is the case when tradition or custom has justified the command and is subject to it. Third, it is legal authority. The legal authority is the case of submission to the command because it is prescribed in the law.

As such, M. Weber saw the form of organization based on such legal authority as bureaucracy. Accordingly, M. Weber has assumed bureaucracy as an organization with a legal authority system based on the concept of legitimacy. Following the characteristics of the authority structure of the bureaucracy, it is necessary to examine the factors that led to the spread of bureaucracy in modern countries.

The premises and grounds for the establishment of bureaucracy with a legal authority system in modern countries include the development of the monetary economy, the quantitative growth and qualitative change of administrative affairs, the technological advantage of the bureaucratic organization, the centralization of accelerated administrative measures and the equalization of social discrimination. In the end, M. Weber saw that these factors created a bureaucracy in modern countries.

Following the consideration of the proposition of bureaucracy, the bureaucracy as a form of organization with a legal authority system based on rationality has the following characteristics.

First, the authority of the bureaucrat is set strictly by law and rules. In other words, the activities performed to achieve the organizational purpose are official duties, which means that they should be allocated according to regulations. At the same time, the mandate required to carry out such duties should also be assigned, and the mandatory means imposed should also be strictly limited by law. These characteristics exist almost exclusively in modern governmental organizations, but only in the most developed capitalist system in the case of enterprises.

Second, the organization follows the principle of hierarchy. All positions form a system of top-down subjugation in which the higher class commands and the lower class subservient by the hierarchy. Thus, the superior shall govern and supervise decisions of the subordinate under the prescribed regulations, which does not mean that there is no jurisdiction of the subordinates at all. The prescribed regulations give powers to subordinates, and this is perpetual.

Third, the execution of the duties is done based on documents, and the property of the organization is separated from the property of the private. Therefore, the document is preserved in the form of original or draft, and the file is regarded as a component of the office.

Fourth, the execution of the duties is specialized so that only those trained as experts can take charge of the work. That is to say, an official within the bureaucracy should have professionalism that has mastered his duties.

Fifth, overall competence is required when performing work. In other words, the work of bureaucrats in the bureaucracy is not an area that can be done as a sideline. In the past, bureaucrats regarded office work as a secondary task, such as concurrent, and did not allocate time and ability to the office entirely. However, in the developed bureaucracy, whether government or private, the task requires a full-time commitment.

Sixth, the execution of the work should be stable and detailed, and it should be done following the rules and standardized operating procedures. Therefore, the bureaucrat as an ideal type should perform the duties by the spirit of formal rationality and impersonality that does not have feelings such as hatred or affection in performing duties.

As shown above, we have examined the propositions and characteristics of bureaucracy. Next, the status of bureaucrats engaged within the bureaucracy can be seen as follows.

First, the government office is a vocation. To have a job as an official, one must possess prescribed education or qualifications or pass a specific examination. So the public office requires full-time employment, which requires all of its abilities, and the bureaucrats can maintain their livelihoods because of their full-time employment.

Second, the status of bureaucrats within the bureaucracy appears in the following forms. In a pure form of bureaucracy, their superiors appoint bureaucrats, and the bureaucrats enjoy high social respect. Thus, the position of appointed bureaucrats is life-long, receiving fixed salaries and pensions. However, the salary paid at this time is not determined by the work performed but is given according to the position and duration of service.

Concerning official salaries, it is common for bureaucrats to be set low, which is due to a strong desire for government posts, not only to be respected in society but also to be stable in income. In particular, bureaucrats are perceived as career positions in the hierarchy, as they can move up and down from lower to higher positions.

The type of organization with the characteristics described is called bureaucracy, and the form of bureaucracy is not the average figure of every organization in the world. This does not mean that the ideal type of bureaucracy does not exist in reality. However, since it is the ideal type that was created to explain the phenomenon, it is meaningful in that it can abstractly deduce the specific appearance of the actual reality through the ideal type.

3) The Dysfunction of Bureaucracy

M. Weber predicted that by establishing a bureaucracy model with a legal authority system based on rationality, he could pursue efficiency, objectivity, consistency, and stability and order of organization. However, the bureaucracy model constructed for this purpose has faced the unintended dysfunctional situation or the bureaucratic pathology. Due to the dysfunction that arises from the characteristics of the bureaucracy itself, the bureaucracy is criticized for its inability to achieve intended effects and, consequently, organizational performance.

Many scholars raised discussions on the dysfunction of bureaucracy, including Robert King Merton, Philip Selznick, Alvin Ward Gouldner, and Victor Alexander Thompson. Despite some differences, there are many similarities in the diagnosis of pathological or dysfunctional conditions of bureaucracy raised by them. Here, instead of examining all the dysfunctional models of the bureaucracy that they would like to elucidate, let us examine the limitations of the bureaucracy in the comprehensive view as follows.

First, there is an increase in formalism. In the bureaucracy, the reliability and conformity of behavior are required. For this, the bureaucracy becomes obsessed with formal rules and procedures. As a result, it causes problems that fall into formalism in which rules are more important than achieving organizational goals. In such a situation where the rules and goals are replaced, only the phenomenon of technicism, red tape, or formalism prevails, resulting in the achievement of organizational goals being pushed back from their priorities.

Second, there is a bureaucrat who wants to accumulate as much of the authority as possible. This bureaucrat typically regards himself as the strongest decision-maker and try to accumulate his authority to the fullest to show off his capability.

Third, there is a widespread tendency to avoid or disperse responsibility spreads. Once the rules and procedures for work are established, responsibilities of the organization members are determined accordingly. However, bureaucratic techniques designed for efficiency easily avoids bureaucratic responsibility. Decisions are made based on the interpretation of superficial phrase rather than the spirit contained in the regulations, and so-called red tape is dominant. The transfer of responsibility is also made in the form of relying on the authority of the supervisor or taking responsibility for the subordinate, or following precedents to avoid responsibility and decision-making. Besides, with the distribution of responsibilities through frequent meetings and negotiations among the various units within the bureaucracy, the original bureaucratic responsibility is lost.

Fourth, problems arise due to delays in decision making. The modern organization is a large organization that is complex and highly interdependent. Thus, the complexity of the decision-making process in a large organization makes it difficult to make a rapid decision.

Fifth, problems are related to bureaucratic interferences. The boundaries of rules established by the bureaucracy cause interference of bureaucrats. For example, the types of disturbances that subordinates do to the supervisor include. They do not provide valuable information to the supervisor or give too much information. So the supervisor cannot eventually use it, or only technically deal with what the supervisor tells them to do and do nothing else. Thus, bureaucrats obstruct the achievement of organizational goals by interfering with them in this way.

Sixth, a bureaucrat considers only his organization essential and has no consideration for other departments, which consequently makes it difficult to coordinate and cooperate because of sectionalism. Sectionalism is because the bureaucracy belongs to a single department for an extended period, resulting in a lack of understanding of other departments, or in competition for the acquisition of resources that are advantageous for the department.

Seventh, the bureaucracy has a fundamental attribute of resistance to change. The main reason for bureaucratic resistance to change is that bureaucracy is inherently precedent-based and status quo. Therefore, it is very complicated to induce or promote the change of the bureaucracy before deliberate and planned efforts.

In addition to the dysfunctions and problems of bureaucracy, for example, the bureaucracy has a variety of dysfunction such as the tendency not to delegate authority, extreme secrecy, the desire for power, the oblivion of public interest, the over-conformity.

3.1.3 The Relevance of Bureaucracy Theory

1) The Critique of Bureaucracy Theory

There are numerous evaluations of bureaucracy theory, among which the evaluation of M. Weber's bureaucracy model can be divided into theoretical and practical. Here, M. Weber's bureaucracy model will be examined in terms of theoretical aspects, and then the limitations of the bureaucracy theory will be examined. However, M. Weber's bureaucracy model has been examined in detail through the dysfunctions of the model, so the criticism of M. Weber will be divided into two aspects as follows.

First, M. Weber's ideal type is mixed with contradictory arguments about the content of the ideal type. For example, the position determines the authority, and on the other hand, it is contradictory to each other that the authority depends on professional and technical ability. Thus, If the superior has higher expertise than a subordinate, the conflict will be resolved, but if not, the authority of the superior in professionalism and hierarchy will collide.

Second, it is a constitutional problem of M. Weber's ideal type. In M. Weber's ideal type, the characteristic that provides consistency and logic between elements is rationality. That is to say, all traits are directed towards rationality. However, there is a problem that the characteristics implied in the bureaucracy do not necessarily guarantee the highest efficiency. The bureaucratic characteristics may be streamlined or inefficient, depending on the situation.

In other words, functional rationality or purposive rationality, which is the ideological basis of M. Weber's bureaucracy, is essential to achieve the goals and values that the organization pursues. As a result, there is a problem that the goals and values of the people who make up the bureaucracy are ignored.

2) The Applicability of Bureaucracy Theory

The concept of old bureaucracy in the political sense of domination by bureaucrats in the early 19th century emerged as a new form of sociological concept by the end of the 19th century. It is a fact that the bureaucracy that emerged in the sociological context concerning this time situation is a new organizational form governed by legal authority based on the rationality of M. Weber.

M. Weber's bureaucracy model began with a sense of the problem to identify how society binds and functions. M. Weber has focused his attention on the legitimacy of the state based on the authority and has found that proper authority has its dynamic power and shape in each dominant cultural environment. As M. Weber argues, the bureaucracy is technically superior to any other form of organization, and that comparing a well-developed bureaucracy with another organization is like comparing a machine with a non-mechanical production.

Just as social science theory began in the times, M. Weber's bureaucracy theory was initially a theory that began in the context of Germany, modeling the Prussian army organization. In other words, the theory of bureaucracy came from the quest for a purposeful rational organization, which was required in the circumstances since the end of the 19th century. Therefore, as the times changed, the revision of bureaucracy was bound to continue.

The contribution of the mechanical bureaucracy theory, including M. Weber's bureaucracy model, was that it provided the most appropriate organizational form for situations in which routine and typical problems had to be handled efficiently in a stable environment.

The bureaucracy model will have limitations in the future where rapid changes in the environment are expected, but the need for a bureaucracy model will persist in an environment in which formal problems need to be managed efficiently. In particular, although there have been many revision models for the bureaucracy model in the meantime, the possibility of applying the bureaucracy model can be seen in that the organizational model that can completely replace the bureaucracy model has not appeared.

Chapter Ⅲ

The Anti Orthodox Public Administration in the Repulsive Period

1. The Story of the Anti Orthodox Public Administration in the Repulsive Years

As the 1930s passed, the administrative states that emerged to cope with the economic panic began to form a backlash against orthodox administration, which accelerated in the 1940s. This period can be seen from 1943 to 1959 when World War II ended.

The core of the opposition to orthodox administration was the fact that politics and administration are not separate from each other, and the non-scientific nature of administrative principles. The critical view that politics and administration, the core of the first rebellion against orthodox administration, cannot be separated was the product of economic panic.

In the process of pushing the New Deal policy to overcome the economic panic, there were reforms to strengthen the leadership of the president along with the expansion of the administrative function. Also, along with the expansion of administration, the function of policy formulation expanded, and the discretion of execution increased. In this process, the power relationship between the legislature and the executive became considerably changed. Unlike in the past, the administration has come to exercise its leadership role in the legislative branch as well as the policy formulation function.

The politics-administration dichotomy, which was the foundation of orthodox administration, faced criticism that it was not only unable to accurately recognize the actual administrative situation of reality but also based on excessive norms while witnessing the changes in the relationship between legislation and administration and between politics and administration. In order to cope with the phenomenon of the superiority of the executive power, the fusion theory of politics-administration or politics-administration monism appeared as a new administrative theory.

When the non-realism of politics-administration dichotomy, which orthodoxy was characterized by, faced such criticism, another rebellion against orthodox administration occurred. The criticism of administrative management theory which explored the principle of value neutrality based on politics-administration dichotomy was raised. Robert Alan Dahl, Dwight Waldo, and Herbert Alexander Simon are the main pillars of criticism on the universality and science of administrative principles.

Besides, in the 1940s, a reflection on the value that the administration should aim at was raised at the same time. For example, D. Waldo exposed the political ideology of administrative principles based on value-neutrality. As a result, the ideology of economy and efficiency, which was the dominant idea in orthodox administration, weakened the forces and instead became interested in the linkage between democratic values and administrative processes in the 1940s.

At that time, there was an atmosphere of recognizing the inevitability of big government, but there was a concern that the big government would hurt democratic values. They were particularly interested in the harmful effects of social and economic control by professional bureaucrats. Along with the criticism of administrative principles, the dispute over the applicability of the science of administration has also been raised in the 1940s.

Finally, in the critical period of orthodox administration, in the field of organizational theory, the human relations theory emerged along with the ecology to study the interaction between organization and environment. Among them, human relations theory, in particular, originated from the theory of the creation of informal organizations and focused on developing management techniques for internal psychology of organizational members.

Meanwhile, due to the expansion of federal bureaucracy following the implementation of the New Deal policy, the role of the government has expanded rapidly since World War II. As a result, there has been a growing concern that there is a danger to the enlargement and strengthening of administrative bodies.

Nevertheless, despite the rapid changes in the environment surrounding the administration, it was the severe problem of this period that the dominant viewpoint of describing and prescribing this environment did not appear in public administration.

In the 1940s, the criticism of orthodox public administration has neutralized the approach based on politics-administration dichotomy and administrative principles that have formed the identity of public administration, but no dominant viewpoint has emerged to replace it. The field of administration and public administration has expanded, but there have been few perspectives and approaches that could integrate the practice and the research of the expanded administrative area.

Due to the lack of a dominant paradigm, in the 1950s, public administration was influenced by various adjacent disciplines such as sociology, anthropology, psychology, business administration, and economics, and became a way of diversification. As a result, public administration has entered a path of diversification. A typical example was that behavioralism influenced the public administration in earnest since World War II. In other words, sociologists and psychologists mainly introduced the behavioral theory and were advocated by Donald W. Smithburg and Victor Alexander Thompson in the field of administration.

The behavioral theory was the central theme of the study to analyze the behavior of individuals within the organization, that is, administrative behavior, through empirical investigation methods, rather than management. Therefore, a group of administrative scholars focused on the scientific explanations of administrative behavior and tried to pursue the administrative principle to explore the regularity of administration. A group of administrative scholars sought to pursue the principle of administration to explore the regularity of administration, which has emerged in various institutions and structures, with the emphasis on the scientific explanation of administrative behavior.

At the same time, decision-making theory also provided another perspective on administrative research in the 1950s. In particular, Herbert A. Simon inherited Chester I. Barnard's theory and developed it into decision-making theory and considered rational decision more important than the administrative value of economy and efficiency.

With the amendment of politics-administration dichotomy, administrative scholars have developed another research tendency to replace scientific management, which has begun to devote to research on the political environment or political reality of administration. Accordingly, case studies were actively utilized in the 1950s, centering on Harold Stein and Frederick Camp Mosher. Case studies have contributed significantly to abandoning the various proverbs that traditional public administration has emphasized and found new ways to solve problems.

Finally, in the 1950s, John Merriman Gaus and Fred W. Riggs began using ecological approaches to study the impact of the environment on administration. In particular, the comparative and developmental administration, which emerged in the late 1950s, has broken through the culture-bound perspective that American public administration has had so far. In other words, after the in the course of the Cold War system between the United States and the Soviet Union after World War II, the United States began economic aid to prevent the erosion of communism in developing countries.

However, as the administrative capacity of these countries was so low that they could not fully reach the aid effectiveness, the comparative administration developed in earnest as a part of the provision of technical aid was studied in the administrative problems of developing countries.

In this way, in the process of administrative and technical aid development in developing countries, the culture-bound nature and the limit of universal validity in American public administration were revealed. As a result, comparative administration research has emerged in order to create a common and reasonable public administration for both developed and underdeveloped countries.

This comparative administration theory has emerged as a part of efforts to improve the scientific nature of public administration and to develop generalized administrative theory through comparative studies on the administration of each country.

2. The Representative Scholars in the Repulsive Years

The following is a description of the contents and characteristics of the administrative theory of this period through the viewpoint of representative scholars before and after the Second World War.

2.1 Abraham Harold Maslow's Needs Hierarchy

Psychologist Abraham Harold Maslow published the famous needs hierarchy called "The Theory of Human Motivation" in the *Psychological Review* in 1943. This theory can be meaningful to the fact that workers are both economic and social beings, one step further from the Hawthorne theory that has been going on since the 1930s. Many scholars assessed his research as a point of view that has promoted development from a new perspective as much as the analysis of M. Weber's bureaucratic structure.

According to A. H. Maslow's needs hierarchy, humans have five goals or basic needs. Physiological need, safety need, belongingness or love need, esteem need, and need for self-actualization. According to the needs hierarchy, an individual pursues the next stage of needs when the needs of the lower level are satisfied, and the already satisfying needs are not the motive to induce human action. In other words, it stops working as a motivational factor for the next action.

Psychological analysis of A. H. Maslow's motivation has made a significant contribution to subsequent research on organizational behavior later. For example, Frederick Herzberg, Douglas Murray McGregor, and Chris Argyris have adopted A. H. Maslow's theory and developed it into motivation theory and organizational behavioral theory.

2.2 Paul Henson Appleby's Politics-Administration Monism

The New Deal and World War II had a significant impact on the theory and practical realm of administration. The problem of depression and oppression caused by the war was initially an economic and military function, but also a substantial administrative situation. So many years of new experiences have raised many questions about what the conventional wisdom of administration is.

Among them, politics-administration dichotomy, which was a prerequisite for the progressive movement, began to lose its feasibility. In short, it meant that accepting the value-free of the administrative process or applying value free to the government was beginning to become impossible.

Despite the efforts of many reformers in the meantime, it has become clear that the government is not a mere business dealt with by corporations, nor is it a value-neutral realm. Therefore, the attack on politics-administration dichotomy begins to emerge.

For example, in 1946, Fritz Morstein Marx criticized the unrealistic nature of politics-administration dichotomy in his edited *Elements of Public Administration*. Also, John Merriman Gaus noted that early administrative scholars were so obsessed with separating politics from the administration that they too perceived the administration as a narrow sense. As a result, he insisted that the administration was far from reality. Many scholars have criticized politics-administration dichotomy, among which the most critical scholar was Paul H. Appleby.

P. H. Appleby served as a director of the New Deal policy in the Roosevelt administration and a dean at Syracuse University. The point he insisted was that the government process, which was not related to politics, was contrary to the experience of the United States. P. H. Appleby argued in his masterpiece, *Big Democracy*, that it is a fictional idea that politics is independent and somehow separate from the administration, breaking down the boundaries between the politics and administration.

He sees political intervention in government as a rather good phenomenon, unlike the views of the progressive reformers. Thus, P. H. Appleby argued that the relationship between politics and administration in the real government is coherent, continuous, and cyclical; it is not appropriate to distinguish between the two and should form a cohesive relationship.

2.3 Herbert Alexander Simon's Logical Positivism

One of the most critical turning points in the development of administrative theory in the 1940s, when World War II ended, was the Herbert Alexander Simon's contribution, who argued that scholars should use a genuinely scientific method in the study of administrative phenomena. H. A. Simon criticized the universality and science of administrative principles and argued that the decision making process was the true essence of administration.

H. A. Simon attempted to claim in "The Proverbs of Administration," a paper published in the *American Public Administration Review* in 1946. In this paper, H. A. Simon criticized the POSDCoRB, which was emphasized by Luther Gulick and others. In other words, he pointed out that there is a mutual contradiction between the principle of specialization, the principle of unity of command, the principle of span of control and the principle of departmentalization, which are representative administrative principles developed by them.

Also, he argued that the principles are merely proverbs that have not undergone scientific experiments, and at best are merely standards or concepts. That is to say, these principles contradict the administrative situation faced by the administrators, and proved that it is inadequate to apply them to the administrative field. In 1947, H. A. Simon later argued, through his masterpiece, the *Administrative Behavior*, that the key to administration is decision making and decision making should be the core of administrative research.

Meanwhile, H. A. Simon developed the concept of bounded rationality on the theoretical foundation of C. I. Barnard. H. A. Simon then later presented a bounded rationality model by further developing the decision-making theory in 1958 in the book *Organization*, which was the co-author of James G. March.

Unlike the early scholars who believed that the scientification of research method could solve all the problems of administration, H. A. Simon was a scholar who recognized the difficulty of scientification as well as the need for scientification of public administration. The term bounded rationality itself describes H. A. Simon's position well. H. A. Simon was the only non-economist to win the Nobel Prize for economics in 1979 through these attempts at decision-making models and organizations.

H. A. Simon indeed had a profound influence on the public administration at the time of World War II. However, at the same time, his arguments for studying public administration have the following limitations.

First, H. A. Simon's perspective did not deviate much from the view of behavioralism. For example, following H. A. Simon's recommendation, there is a problem that the study of administration should be conducted only for those who have no organization because the internal environment, motivation, and informal human relations is the basis of the analysis.

Second, it can only lead to the phenomenon that the conservatism becomes strengthened because it focuses on analyzing the phenomenon existing or revealed. This phenomenon falls into conservatism, which only deals with problems that can be solved based on the reliability of measurements rather than political and social importance if one excludes value judgment and only studies logic things or concentrate on the reliability of methods.

In particular, conservatism is at considerable risk of neglecting the formation of new goals or possible alternatives in combination with H. A. Simon's underlying assumption of human rationality, bounded rationality. As a result, there is a problem that reform or change is easy to ignore naturally.

2.4 Robert Alan Dahl's Science of Administration

While the logical positivist H. A. Simon argued for finding empirically identified principles, he emphasized the introduction of natural scientific research methods in public administration research, while on the other hand, there was a serious debate about the relevance for the science of administration.

The first debate on the relevance of the science of administration was by Robert Alan Dahl, who had a serious question about the feasibility of establishing the science of administration. In particular, at a time when the apparent boundary between political science and public administration collapsed due to the collapse of the politics-administration dichotomy, R. A. Dahl published "The Science of Public Administration" in the *American Public Administration Review* in 1947.

In the context of the collapse of the boundary between political science and public administration, R. A. Dahl proposed the following conditions for the scientificization of public administration, that is, for the study of public administration, to have its own identity. First, it should be accompanied by an understanding of the complexity of human behavior. Second, administrative phenomena should deal with the issue of normative value. Third, scholars should consider the relationship between the administration and the social environment.

In particular, he emphasized the importance of interrelationships between the administration and social environment and asserted that public administration as a science would be empty unless a comparative study was the basis of public administration.

As R. A. Dahl predicted, the public administration led comparative public administration to the sub-specialty of public administration in the 1950s and 1960s, but there was little the department of public administration to educate comparative public administration. He also anticipated the difficulties that public administration should face when it wants to remain a part of political science.

However, unlike R. A. Dahl's concerns, the public administration programs were separated from the department of political science and the department of business administration by the 1970s, and the tendency to be established as an independent department became clear. However, in the United States, public administration programs remain a specialized area of political science or business administration.

R. A. Dahl held a stance of behavioralism, but it was somewhat different from Herbert A. Simon's logical positivism. Unlike H. A. Simon, who emphasizes decision-making aspects, he stressed the need for comparative research for social relations with the administration and generalization of the administrative theory. In other words, there is a clear difference in the attempt to complement the social and macro aspects that are overlooked in behaviorism. To this end, R. A. Dahl emphasized the importance of comparative research as well as the importance of a situational approach to administration.

He emphasized not only the efforts to extract different phenomena, characteristics, or common elements, but also the efforts to extract similar phenomena, characteristics, or different elements; as a result, referring to the inevitability of comparative research. Besides, R. A. Dahl's claim that the position of a normative value in administrative studies should be apparent was later accepted to some extent in public administration due to the emergence of policy science and new public administration.

However, despite R. A. Dahl's contribution, his argument has several problems.

First, there is an inherent contradiction as long as it maintains a behavioral approach from the methodological point of view.

Second, as long as normative value research implies preserving and strengthening only the existing values as shown in the study of R. A. Dahl, it will, in essence, result in similar results to the conservatism of behavioralists such as H. A. Simon.

Third, the argument that human nature and behavior in the administrative domain should be well understood and predictable is desirable. However, there is a problem of how to choose a view or perspective on human nature. Therefore, this problem is accompanied by a methodological problem that data and theory cannot exist independently of each other.

2.5 Verne B. Lewis's Budget Theory

At the time of active discussion of the scientification and identity of public administration around World War II, efforts to develop and consolidate new techniques in the field of budgeting have also begun.

In this atmosphere, Verne B. Lewis, who served as a federal budget officer, published a paper in the *American Public Administration Review* in 1952, entitled "Toward a Theory of Budgeting" to raise rationality in the budget area by presenting the so-called theory of alternative budgeting.

In this paper, V. B. Lewis presented his solution to the basis of decision for the allocation of public expenditure, which was proposed by Valdimer Orlando Key, Jr. 12 years ago. In other words, if V. O. Key proposed the need to deal with the budget based on an economic approach, V. B. Lewis put forward the basic proposition for the economic analysis of the budget from the point of view beyond V. O. Key's proposition.

It is necessary to examine the relative value of the budget, incremental analysis, relative effectiveness, and these three propositions should be in the basis of the budget system to become a budget based on economic analysis. To this end, V. B. Lewis has suggested the need for an alternative budget system.

The alternative budgeting system, which V. B. Lewis preferred, is a means to overcome the traditional budget accounting system, which focuses on the controls pursued by the line-item budgeting system. Thus, the alternative budgeting system was designed to measure the level of program services or goals that are in line with changes in funding, as compared to the traditional line-item budgeting system.

In particular, the concept of relative value at the core of V. B. Lewis's budget theory, the rational comparison of budget alternatives, and the method of budget cuts have significantly impact on budgetary systems for rational resource allocation, such as the Planning Programming Budgeting Systems(PPBS) in the 1960s and Zero-based budgeting(ZBB) in the 1970s.

V. B. Lewis showed that economic propositions could be applied to in the process of comparative analysis and selection of budget alternatives to find a rational decision-making basis for budget allocation. This discussion has contributed further to enhancing rationality in administration. Thus, the characteristics of V. B. Lewis's research in attempting to make an economical approach to the budget are, in a nutshell, a series of efforts to rationalize administration in a broad context and to rationalize budget decision and operation in a narrow context

However, V. B. Lewis himself admitted the limitations of the economic approach by admitting that non-economic and irrational factors were involved in the budgetary process without being eliminated. In other words, V. B. Lewis, who can be called a realist, had no choice but to admit that factors such as price, prejudice, regional traits, and politics influenced budget decisions. However, V. B. Lewis hoped that a budget system would emerge to overcome these non-economical and irrational factors.

2.6 Dwight Waldo's Administrative State

At the time when criticism of universality and scientificity of administrative principles was vigorously developed around Herbert A. Simon, Dwight Waldo was the scholar who raised questions about the relevance of administrative principles and the scientificity emphasized by positivists.

2.6.1 The Criticism of Efficiency

The first problem that D. Waldo approached was the criticism of orthodox administration. In his book *Administrative State*, published in 1948 by revising his doctoral dissertation, He made a grueling attack on the concept of the gospel of efficiency that scholars had evangelized in public administration until before World War II. He criticized Luther Gulick's ideas and theories, especially among evangelicals for efficiency, and argued that there was a fundamental flaw in orthodox administration. As a result, he revealed that there was no true principle in orthodox administration.

D. Waldo criticized the unfairness of the fundamentalist theories of traditional classical theories and emphasized that the focus of administrative research should shift to finding a rational action in pursuit of efficiency. Besides, D. Waldo presented democracy as a new value that the administration should pursue. In particular, he recalled that scholars misinterpret democracy concerning relation to traditional values such as efficiency and authority.

For example, D. Waldo understood that in the context of democracy as a new administrative value, the Hawthorne experiment centered primarily on the Elton Mayo was an effort to find alternatives from a human aspect to improve the illness of industrial organizations based on scientific management theory. However, ultimately, organizational humanitarianism and human relations studies were seen as merely efforts to find the means necessary for efficiency.

D. Waldo's idea was that if management theories, such as organizational humanitarianism, were ultimately aimed at pursuing a higher despotism, then even if benevolent paternalism were in the basis of management theories, such management theories were not seeking a healthy functioning democratic system. Thus, D. Waldo argued that the development of management theories developed in the private sector did not coincide with the development of democratic administration theory. D. Waldo saw a severe problem in applying the principles developed in the private sector in particular to the public sector.

D. Waldo argued that the concept of efficiency rather than democracy in the realm of public administration had been recognized as a significant value because the value emphasized in private administration has entered the realm of public administration without any filtering device.

As such, D. Waldo warned that there is a severe problem in applying the principles developed in the private sector to the public sector. In particular, the reason for this is that, as seen in the traditional administration, the progressive reform movement, it is based on the belief that it is desirable to pursue efficiency even at the expense of democracy.

In conclusion, D. Waldo emphasized that scholars should make a desirable link between democracy as a goal and efficiency as a means in order to revise the wrong value system and to promote the development of democratic administrative theory.

2.6.2 The Criticism of Positivism

The second problem that D. Waldo approached was the critique of positivism that began to fade in the public administration, revealing the political ideology of the value-neutral administrative principle on which orthodox administrative scholars based. D. Waldo identified public administration as an entity with value-loaded characteristics, not value-neutral, as claimed in orthodox administration.

Because administration should be viewed as an ideological character in which the administration has already involved value, it is impossible to think of a value-free administration and that science-oriented administration is not capable of solving social problems.

D. Waldo thus posed a problem to the science that was emphasized in positivism, in which he saw that the essence of the science was not made up only by the spread of common sense, acquisition, or empiricism. In other words, D. Waldo understood that scientific theory could only be achieved by internal creeds, not merely by the accumulation of data and repetition of cases. Therefore, D. Waldo criticized the positivists for overlooking it.

However, D. Waldo criticized the scientific nature that was in vogue at the time, but D. Waldo did not entirely deny the methodology of natural science. D. Waldo emphasized that although humans exist in a natural order and that natural scientific methods can approach a series of administrative problems, but the problem of administration is ultimately is bound to be deeply connected with values. These values include individualism, democracy, freedom and equality, and peace.

In a similar vein, D. Waldo realistically recognized the mechanical efficiency claimed by logical positivists and behavioralists. Besides, D. Waldo argued for the concept of conciliated efficiency that compromises and harmonizes the two, in the sense that relative efficiency, considering the specificity of value culture, also exists.

2.7 Charles Edward Lindblom's Incrementalism

Charles Edward Lindblom's work served as a milestone marking the end of the postwar era because the most crucial part of the government's efforts is policy and decision-making. C. E. Lindblom showed great interest in the policy-making process, while political scientists showed interest in political ideology, political philosophy, political system, and power structure, and focused mainly on the policy output and policy-making system.

Policy decision pursues two mutually different values of efficiency and responsiveness to citizen control. While efficiency emphasizes the analytical aspects of policy-making, responsiveness to citizen control emphasizes political aspects. Thus, C. E. Lindblom saw the policy-making process as having a gradual character in conflict and harmony between efficiency and responsiveness.

As a result, C. E. Lindblom supported strategic policy decisions that perceived analysis as an element of political interaction and subordinated it to political interactions rather than scientific policy decisions that emphasized analysis as an alternative to politics. Strategic policy decisions mean recognizing the limitations of human cognitive ability and grasping policy decision as a political process.

C. E. Lindblom raised to claim in 1959 on "The Science of Muddling Through," published in the *American Public Administration Review*. C. E. Lindblom criticized the rational model of the decision process emphasized by the government in this paper and refuted the claim that a rational process that took all information into account made most decisions.

Instead, C. E. Lindblom saw political events or environments more influence that decision making than by the will or intention of policy-makers. The incrementalism emphasized by C. E. Lindblom not only describes the policy decisions in reality but also includes the normative aspects of how decisions should be made. In other words, by developing the concept of bounded rationality in decision making, he advocated the incrementalism that gradual change is achieved rather than comprehensive reform in the political process.

C. E. Lindblom published the "Still Muddling, Not Yet Through," which revised the paper in 1979. His incrementalism was then the cornerstone of the development of management science and policy science in the 1960s. Besides, C. E. Lindblom's analytical perspective also facilitated the study of disciplines in the boundary between politics and public administration.

The most considerable influence of C. E. Lindblom on administrative theory is incrementalism. C. E. Lindblom criticized rationalist decision-making theory and emphasized that the policy decisions made in actual administrative phenomena are made gradually. C. E. Lindblom's model of incrementalism has pointed out the problems of rationalism and emerged from the standpoint of reflecting the characteristics of a real-life policy decision so that it can reduce the risk burden and can also guarantee the conservatism of the policy system.

However, C. E. Lindblom's model of incrementalism reveals its limitations in that the possibility that the incrementalism itself becomes the logic of vested rights despite these characteristics can be a hindrance to reform. Especially since the incremental fashion virtually decides policy decisions that are generally made, it is criticized that incrementalism is not a prescriptive theory but rather an explanatory theory.

3. The Representative Theory in the Repulsive Years

The representative administrative theories that emerged in the repulsive period of public administration are behavioralism theory and comparative administration theory. The background, characteristics, and contents of the theories that led to the formation of these theories are as follows.

3.1 Behavioralism Theory

The concept of behavioral theory or behavioralism is ambiguous and has a wide variety of origins. According to James C. Miller, the term 'behavior' may have been used in the past, but in politics, it was used by American political scientists during World War I. Nevertheless, J. C. Miller sees the beginning of the publication of a book in 1928 by journalist F. Kent using this term.

However, the first example in which the term 'behavior' was officially used in the United States was the *Administrative Behavior* published by Herbert A. Simon in 1947. Moreover, since 1949, the term behavioralism or behavioral science has begun to be used in social sciences.

3.1.1 The Background of Behavioralism Theory

Behavioralism began to appear in politics for the first time, replacing traditionalism, which was the primary approach to political science until the 1920s. Traditionalism was the primary research trend that dominated political science. Although it was a disadvantage to be biased toward a somewhat excessive idealism, traditionalism held a firm position in that historical consciousness was on the basis of traditionalism in analyzing social phenomena.

However, the traditional method of research was far from what we are talking about today. In other words, the positions and theories claimed by traditionalism were often an arbitrary argument rather than scientific theories in modern terms. As a result, behavioralism that emphasizes scientific theories has emerged in the context of replacing traditionalism. In this context, the reasons for the widespread proliferation of behavioralism in political science are as follows.

First, the widespread dissatisfaction with the academic status of political science has led to the adoption and diffusion of behavioralism as a new research trend. For example, not only was the professionalism of political scientists not highly regarded by government officials, but traditionalism, which at that time was the dominant research trend, was too incompetent to explain new systems such as fascism, national socialism, and socialism. As a result, the skeptic atmosphere about the descriptive academic characteristics of traditionalism has spread, and behavioralism has become a new research trend.

Second, the reflection of the fact that the United States has had little effect on technology aid or economic aid programs for new countries since World War II accelerated the introduction of behavioralism. Political science was therefore required to find regularities which are cross-cultural and transnational.

Third, changes in research trends began to emerge due to the influences of European sociologists who immigrated to the United States during the 1930s and 1940s. For example, logical positivism, which had a profound influence on behavioralism, was imported at this time, and behavioralism based on logical positivism wide-spread. Finally, the spread of opinion polls and the development of research techniques after World War II contributed to the spread of behavioralism.

As mentioned, in contrast to the reason that the behavioralism was introduced and spread into the political science, in the case of the administration, there is a part that overlaps with that of the political science, but the cause was more straightforward. Behavioralism, which began with H. A. Simon as its starting point, had its aim in the scientificization of administration.

The introduction of behavioralism, which was raised by criticizing that the principles that the current orthodox administration had been believed to be merely a proverb that was not verified, was the scientificization of public administration itself. In this respect, behavioralism in public administration has developed as part of a scientific movement based on logical positivism influenced by European empiricism and positivism.

3.1.2 The Content and Characteristic of Behavioralism Theory

1) The Meaning of Behavioralism

The conceptualization of behavioralism was attempted by Robert A. Dahl, whose conceptualization of behavioralism was done in two aspects.

First, he viewed behavioralism as a protest movement within the political science of the United States. The reason why he viewed behavioralism as a protest movement is because it has emerged as an alternative to the dissatisfaction with the performance of the historical, philosophical, technological and institutional approaches that the traditional American political science has tried.

Second, he saw a series of attempts to make political science more scientific as behavioralism. A series of attempts began with the belief that there could be new methodologies and approaches to develop further political science, which could help to form a systematic theory of political science.

In short, behavioralism that emerged in the realm of political science was not aimed at pursuing a better life, but at portraying and understanding political phenomena realistically and predicting something through it.

While R. A. Dahl conceptualized the behavioralism as such, he raised fundamental questions about the possibility of improving the study of political science through the behavioral approach, which was divided into three views.

The first position was supported by the Social Science Research Council report over 1944 and 1945 and by David Easton's *Political*

System published in 1953, which said that behavioralism would contribute to improving the research of political science. In particular, according to D. Easton, traditionalists carried out the study by viewing the system as an entity away from the individuals, while behavioral studies are the work of attracting humans to the center of research attention. From this point of view, he argued that behavioralism is a concept that has more meaning than an atmosphere.

The second position was Alfred de Grazia, who took a skeptical view of this possibility. He took the position that behavioralism was not more than an interdisciplinary focus, a quantification, an effort on a new methodology, a realism opposed to idealism, empiricism contrary to the deductive system, and the like.

The third position is that while emotional consent is given to R. A. Dahl, behavioralism is merely an attempt to make the empirical component of discipline more scientific. In other words, behavioralism is merely an approach aimed at enhancing understanding of politics by explaining the practical aspects of politics through general rules and modern empirical science. David Bicknell Truman supported this view. He saw that behavioralism was merely an orientation aimed at describing all the phenomena of government by observable or observed human behavior.

In conclusion, there are various perspectives on whether or not scholars should see behavioralism as a new trend or tendency that is meaningful in developing political or administrative research. Therefore, it is a difficult task to define the nature of behavioralism. However, despite various questions about the nature of behavioralism, the common ground among them was that the ultimate purpose of behavioralism was to enhance scientific character.

2) The Orientation and Characteristics of Behavioralism

To understand the specific details of behavioralism, first of all, the direction or orientation that behavioralism pursues is as follows.

First, behavioralism pursues science capable of prediction and explanation. The nature of science is closely related to biology rather than physics or chemistry, and it is necessary to avoid purely descriptive studies to develop political knowledge.

Second, behavioralism focuses on research only on what can be observed and what is done, if not exclusive. In this respect, political science should abstain from the institutional approach.

Third, the data should be organized into quantified, and quantitative data must be on the basis of the results.

Fourth, research should be theory-oriented and theory-seeking. The ultimate purpose of behavioral research is to attempt to generalize the phenomenon accurately and to show its relevance.

Fifth, behavioralism pursues a pure research position. Thus, behavioral political science must abandon applied research aimed at solving specific social problems.

Sixth, the authenticity of the value problem is not scientifically verifiable. Examples of value problems include democracy, equality, and freedom. Thus, the value issue is a problem outside the realm pursued by behavioralism. So behavioralists should not engage in the significant issues.

Seventh, behavioralism pursues an interdisciplinary position.

Eighth, behavioralism is more self-aware and consistently critical of the methodology.

However, the debate with traditionalists about the orientation pursued by behavioralism has been tedious since 1930 when behavioralism was introduced into politics. Then in the 1960s, by the way, David Easton summarized the characteristics of behavioralism through the behavioral credo, the tedious debate between traditionalism and behavioralism ended. As the characteristics of behavioralism, D. Easton suggested eight factors: regularity, verification, technique, quantification, value, systematization, pure science, and integration.

First, behavioralism seeks to find regularities. Behavioralism is to increase the predictability by finding uniformities on the premise that there will be certain uniformities in the social phenomenon centered on human behavior. In other words, behavioralism is to pursue theories or generalizations that can explain and predict the phenomenon. In response, traditionalists argue that the reality of political phenomena is unique and not uniform. Moreover, they argued that human behavior is not something that will be studied objectively, whether it is individual or social.

Second, behavioralism makes verification a necessary condition. In behavioralism, knowledge is composed of pre-verification propositions, which should, of course, be empirically verified. All evidence must be made by observation or the like. However, while the verification of the reality may be possible on the surface, traditionalists argue that most social phenomena are hidden behind the more complicated and unclear bodies, making it doubtful whether observation can identify them.

Third, behavioralism requires techniques. In particular, techniques are needed to ensure the validity, reliability, and comparability of data. However, data is often inaccurate and unreliable, which is a problem. In particular, traditionalists criticize that what is called data in the social sciences are not objective and that relying on techniques at the expense of content does not improve the quality of research.

Fourth, behavioralism is based on quantification. To obtain precise and accurate knowledge from complex social phenomena, it is sometimes necessary to convert ambiguous qualitative information into quantitative information. At this time, strict measurement and data manipulation must follow. However, the problem of quantification is not an easy subject.

Even if the measurement is impossible or what is not measurable is manipulated or analyzed in numbers, its true meaning will disappear. Therefore, the problem of quantification is the crux of behavioralism and also the area to be most careful. In response to such quantification, traditionalists criticize the behavioralists for pursuing purposes that cannot be achieved. In other words, they argue, it is only a futile attempt to quantify something that cannot be quantified.

Fifth, behavioralism pursues value neutrality. Scientific inquiry thoroughly excludes the intervention of value in order to maintain original objectivity. However, there is a problem that the tendency to value cannot help but intervene when dealing with reality in reality. So the issue of value neutrality is also the fiercest part of the debate between traditionalists and behavioralists.

Behavioralists say that ethical evaluations and empirical explanations are different. Thus, facts and values should be logically separated, and scientific research has nothing to do with moral or ethical issues. Traditionalists, on the other hand, point to the fact that significant political issues often involve moral and ethical issues, and that political science does not tolerate not expressing a position on the issue of right and wrong. As such, traditionalists say that as researchers, they can never rule out value preferences in their research.

Sixth, behavioralism pursues systematization. Knowledge is obtained systematically from a behavioral point of view. A verifiable hypothesis should be derived deductively from the theoretically connected concepts, and structure of propositions, which are proven through new evidence in the world of experience, and the theory is established. In summary, behavioral research should be theory-oriented. On the other hand, traditionalists talk about value theory, and there is a difference that they are particularly interested in causal theory.

Seventh, behavioralism pursues pure science. It means that not all studies are immediately applied or reflected in policies at a practical level. In other words, pure knowledge that solidifies the foundations of applied science may be needed on the other hand. In contrast, traditionalists argue that if a theory cannot be applied to a political problem in society, or if it does not help to find a solution, then such a theory is not worth it. Thus, traditionalists argue that the noble purpose of social scientists lies in finding ways to solve the difficulties that exist in society.

Eighth, behavioralism pursues integration. Behavioralism advocates a multidisciplinary position, a link among disciplines. Behavioralists try to integrate and utilize the methods and theories of other disciplines, and the findings obtained from the research, without confining themselves to the realm of individual sciences.

Traditionalists take mostly the same stand on integration, but not on the same page as political scientists have been borrowing techniques or methodologies developed in overly different social sciences.

3) The Compositional Content of Behavioralism

As above, traditionalism and behavioralism are different in their orientation and characteristics. As a result, the content that constitutes behavioralism varies widely, depending on the perspectives or development process, making it difficult to describe it clearly. However, behavioralism, in public administration, generally refers to the logical positivism of Herbert Alexander Simon. From logical positivism, the composition of behavioralism is as follows.

First, behavioralism focuses on the behavior patterns of organizational members of the organization. They focus their research on organizational behavior rather than on the structural aspects of the organization. In other words, they will grasp the administrative phenomenon through the behavior style of the administrators. However, focusing on research in behavior style does not neglect or ignore collective phenomena.

Instead, scholars like H. A. Simon emphasize the importance of the group by saying that regulating human behavior is the norm or spirit of the group he belongs to rather than the psychological inside of the human being. The only thing they neglected was the institutions and structures that were far from human behavior. They value the role of the organization or group within the scope of explaining human behavior.

Second, behavioralism argues that value should be distinguished from fact, and value should be excluded from the subject of study. They claim that public administration should increase scientific quality by adopting a value-neutral research method like natural science. Public administration is aimed and fulfills its practical value by finding the best way to achieve the goal, and it cannot and should not deal with any more value-loaded problems.

In other words, they should not deal with such valuable and ethical issues as to why and how in the administrative phenomenon. It should not address the value and ethical issues such as what to do and what to do in the administrative phenomenon.

They argue that all theories must be verifiable and that when there is no possibility of verification, they are fiction and not theory. They say that administrative phenomena are thoroughly facts, not value phenomena or ethical phenomena.

Third, behavioralism prefers a quantitative approach or technique. It is easy to think that the behavioral approach is usually the same as the quantitative approach, but in methodologies, the two approaches are only likely to be binding but not the same. Since behavioral approach tracks and explains the whole through a set of individual actions in original, it is inevitable to use quantitative approaches or techniques.

In other words, quantitative techniques are almost inevitable in this process because they describe the whole phenomenon by aggregating individual phenomena. Notably, the behavioral approach emphasizes the verifiability of the theory, which is the quantitative method that enables verification.

Fourth, behavioralism has a comprehensive scientific character because it focuses on explaining human behavior. A comprehensive explanation of human behavior requires the help of psychology, sociology, and cultural anthropology, emphasizing interdependence with these disciplines. In particular, the behavioral approach emphasizes administrative culture because it focuses on the structure of consciousness, a pattern of behavior, a way of thinking, value system, and preference of the bureaucrats.

Fifth, H. A. Simon, a behavioralist, identifies the administrative phenomenon as a decision-making process. The administrative organization is a unit of decision-making as an aggregate, and the administrator is making decisions within this category. Decision-making also links to the behavior of individual administrators. Here, the administrative organization functions as a unit of the decision-making situations in which administrators make decisions.

Moreover, all administrators' behaviors are the same as or directly connected with the selected action of the alternative. The scientific explanation of an organization is a description of what decisions an organizational man makes and how those factors influence decisions.

Sixth, behavioralism identifies administration as a dynamic interplay between individuals with various needs or between individuals and groups. At this time, human beings have both economic and psychological desires. Therefore, administrative phenomena are bound to be at odds all the time and are entangled with complicated elements.

3.1.3 The Emergence and Characteristic of Post-Behavioralism

Behavioralism, which had been in its heyday since World War II, began to set its limitations in the 60s. As an alternative, post-behavioralism agreed with the direction in which behavioralism was oriented, only to increase its relevance and prescription, which were pointed out as the limitations of behavioralism.

As already mentioned, the epistemological basis of behavioralism is based initially on positivism and ultimately on the empiricism of the United Kingdom. There are many theories about the nature of behavioralism with this epistemological background. One of them is post-behavioralism, which emerged according to David Easton's claim. Post-behavioralism criticizes behavioralism for overconfidence in logical positivism and logical empiricism. However, the criticism of behavioralism by post-behavioralism should not confuse traditionalism with post-behavioralism.

While traditionalism has denied the validity of the behavioral approach and paid attention to the classical traditions of political science, there is a difference in that post-behavioralists acknowledge the achievements of the behavioral era and merely attempt to push political science to the new horizon.

As D. Easton pointed out, post-behavioralism is a movement that aims to promote political science in a new direction by adding future orientation in a more or less complementary context, rather than denying behavioralism. So D. Easton says that post-behavioralism is not a reaction but a real revolution. In other words, post-behavioralism is not preservation but a reform, a movement, and a new intellectual tendency.

As a movement, post-behavioralism calls for two things: relevance and action. D. Easton enumerates the seven primary attributes of post-behavioralism, describing them as the credo of relevance. The attributes of proposed by D. Easton are as follows.

First, post-behavioralism emphasizes that substance should take precedence over the technique, and post-behavioralism also agrees that delicate research tools are needed. Nevertheless, more importantly, it is a matter of purpose to pursue. Scientific research should cure urgent social problems, and if there is no meaning or relevance, then it is not necessary to do such research. So that is why the slogan in the post-behavioralism may be better ambiguity than accuracy without relevance.

Second, post-behavioralism should focus on social change rather than social conservation, where behavioralism has emphasized. Behavioralists have strengthened the ideology of conservatism through incremental fluctuations without taking into account the broad context of the society in which they live. On the other hand, post-behavioralism claims to abandon such an ideology.

Third, behavioralism has focused on activities such as analyzing in the laboratory while ignoring the political reality like the beast. Therefore, if political scientists are not responsible for this phenomenon, politics is not worth the existence. In this sense, post-behavioralism emphasizes the practicality of politics.

Fourth, even behavioralists cannot be regarded as completely denying the role of value, but the critical point is that if knowledge is used for the right purpose, a value should now return to the central position of research.

Fifth, post-behavioralism emphasizes the intellectual role of political scholars: that is, political scientists should protect human values in a civilized society.

Sixth, in the post-behavioralism, if intellectuals understand social problems and they belong together in these matters, intellectuals should do something to solve them with action. In other words, knowing means having the responsibility to move into action, and also acting means being involved in restructuring society.

Seventh, in the post-behavioralism, the politicization of the profession is inevitable. That is to say, the politicization of political scholars and universities is inevitable and desirable.

In conclusion, the direction in which post-behavioralism pursues is that the research should be relevant in understanding social issues. Also, D. Easton emphasized that political scientists should be able to present solutions to social problems and play a leading role in enabling scholars to make desirable social changes.

3.1.4 The Relevance of Behavioralism Theory

1) The Limitations of Behavioralism Theory

There have been many points of view about the theoretical limitations of behavioralism by traditionalists and post-behavioralists. Therefore, the limitations and constraints of behavioralism are as follows.

First, behavioralism is criticized for paying attention mainly to the general and regular nature of human behavior. Thus, while observing and explaining the objective behavior of the human outer appearance, there is a limit to grasping the true inner meaning of the behavior. In particular, it is not appropriate to separate values and facts and to exclude value judgments, and it is all the more problematic that social scientists cannot help but have any preferences or ethical positions in their research.

Second, it is a criticism that behavioralism has alleviated the utility and validity of social phenomena. As a result, it is a criticism that because behavioralism has dealt with only the world of objectively existent facts, it has been mired in empirical conservatism and turning a blind eye to the problem of social change.

Third, it is a criticism that behavioralism tends to establish a model that is inflexible and thus to harm the suitability of research.

Fourth, behavioralists tend to create jargon and interfere with communication. The theory pursued in behavioralism is right in the theory itself and may contribute to the improvement of scientific quality in public administration, but it does not help much in solving social problems.

Fifth, it is a criticism that behavioralists cannot make useful policy contributions. Critics point out that when public administration or politics cannot deal with the value problem, it can not help to solve the real social problem because it can not give any direction or prescription.

2) The Applicability of Behavioralism Theory

Despite these criticisms of behavioralism, broadly-defined behavioralism theory today is trying to contribute to policy contributions by overcoming constraints of their own with sophisticated methods and relevant theories.

Behavioralism has indeed contributed to the field of study despite the many problems that behavioralism has and its content will dominate the thought of academic research for a long time in the future, making some modifications according to the demands of the times. However, it does not mean that it will be as it is in the original state of behavioralism, but it will have to undergo many transformations.

In conclusion, the contribution that behavioralism has brought can be viewed in two main respects. In other words, the performance of behavioralism has achieved remarkable growth in theory formation and technique of research. Among them, the performance of behavioralism, in particular, is found to be more valuable in the area of research techniques. Today, many research techniques used in social sciences are considered to be the result of behavioralism, and there is no big deal, so we can evaluate the contribution of behavioralism in that it is not too much.

3.2 Comparative Administration Theory

3.2.1 The Background of Comparative Administration Theory

The interest in comparative studies in public administration began to gain momentum after World War II. Before that, there was little interest in comparative studies between countries, as most countries focused primarily on improving the efficiency of administration, mainly on domestic issues.

However, after World War II, the situation started to change. Many colonial governments were newly independent, and the power landscape of the great powers changed utterly. The United States and the Soviet Union, which formed the united front during the war, split into ideological differences and entered the so-called Cold War era.

The world has been reorganized into the East and West camps centered on the United States and the Soviet Union, and the great powers have been competing to put the new country in its sphere of influence. As a result, interest in the political system and the administrative system of the new country was bound to rise significantly. The competition between the East and West camps, which try to place the new countries under their influence, has been fiercely developed from the process of forming the political and administrative structures of these countries.

The Soviet Union was bent on establishing its communist ideology and system within the new country, and the United States and other Western countries also provided various supports to spread the democratic system. In terms of administrative organizations and institutions, advanced powers are also competing to make the new country adopt its model, with the United States exerting significant influence against the backdrop of economic aid.

However, economic aid and administrative support faced many unexpected problems rather than achieving the desired results. The massive amount of aid has been exploited to encourage wasteful factors such as corruption and rort rather than being used for economic development or life improvement of new countries. Besides, the political and administrative system of developed countries did not meet the conditions of the new country, resulting in side effects and trial and error.

As a result, scholars felt the necessity of doubt and review of the Western administrative theory and the administrative system of advanced countries. They became skeptical as to whether it was the most rational and advanced theory and system, and they began to take a step further and focus on what factors Western administrative patterns and theories did not function appropriately in new and developing countries.

To identify the factors, it became necessary to have a deeper understanding and knowledge of the cultural traditions and administrative behaviors of Asian and African countries in particular. As the need has become urgent, the number of scholars with experience in the administration of new or underdeveloped countries has increased, and comparative administrative research has begun to be actively promoted. In particular, many scholars had the opportunity to participate in administrative consultations or education training as part of the so-called technical assistance for countries that received the United States foreign aid.

They have come to realize that in order for aid to the new countries to be used efficiently, it is essential not only to provide material support but also to improve administrative capabilities and management skills. In addition to the emergence of comparative administrative research, the significant factors that led to the development of comparative administrative research as a movement are as follows.

First, it is the scientific endeavor of the administration. Conventional administration has been studied by technical, static, and normative methods based mainly on the American experience. However, the search for a new theory stimulated the study of comparative administration as criticism was raised against it. Also, as a result of applying the administration of the United States to the administration of the developing countries, they found that it was very different from the expectation. Therefore, the specificity of administration is formed according to the historical, political, and social conditions of each country. So, it is necessary to study the administration comprehensively and comparatively.

Second, it is the proliferation of United States foreign aid program. After World War II, as the United States provided economic aid and technical assistance to developing countries, knowledge of the administrative problems of the target countries became necessary. Many administrative experts participated in this aid plan, which raised interest in comparative administration.

Third, it is the influence of comparative politics. After World War II, comparative politics has shifted from an institutional approach to a functional approach. So the focus of research has also shifted from the Western-centric perspective to the developing countries.

First of all, comparative politics was able to get help in the data because the research was done before the comparative public administration promptly, and comparative politics stimulated the development of comparative administration by including a comparison of the administrative system in the comparative study of the political system. In other words, comparative public administration mostly followed the analysis method of comparative politics in general. For example, theoretical models and concepts of comparative politics, whether conscious or unconscious, are introduced, and the same scholars are participating in the formation of the theory.

Fourth, the activities of the comparative administration Group are mentioned. The Comparative Administration Group(CAG), a sub-committee of the American Society for Public Administration, has contributed to comparative administrative research by holding annual summer seminars under the guidance of F. W. Riggs, supported by the Ford Foundation.

3.2.2 The Content and Characteristic of Comparative Administration Theory

1) The Concept and Purpose of Comparative Administration Theory

Two aspects should be considered in advance in attempting to define the concept of comparative administration theory.

First, it is a matter of the field of comparative administration. The scope of comparative administration is relatively broad and can be carried out across various subjects. In this respect, comparative administration theory has been treated as a synonym for administrative research in neighboring cultures or neighboring countries, for reasons that are contingent rather than logical.

Of course, comparative studies on administration cannot be confined to comparing only different cultural environments or administrative systems in the nation. However, the focus of attention today is not to deny that administrative systems and administrative behavior are cross-cultural comparisons. However, there is no denying that what is at the center of attention today is the comparison of administrative institutions and administrative behaviors on a cross-cultural level.

Second, the question of how to define comparative administration in terms of an approach of research is raised. It is not enough to list the reality of the administrative systems in various countries. As Fred W. Riggs has stated, the concept of comparison should be used exclusively in empirical or nomothetic studies in a strict sense. Although this position is overly narrow-minded, comparative research should adopt a scientific approach to theory building.

Accordingly, the concept of comparative administration can be divided into a broad meaning and a narrow sense. The conceptualization of the comparative administration attempted in the broader context is the concept definition of the comparative administration group(CAG), which was established as a subcommittee of the American Society for Public Administration.

This research group defined the concept of comparative administration as a collection of administrative theories that can be applied to diverse cultures and institutions of various countries, and a set of factual data that can be verified and developed by these theories. On the other hand, empirical and nomothetic studies limit the conceptualization of comparative administration in a narrow context. In other words, normative and individual studies are not strictly comparative studies, and the term comparison can be used only in cross-cultural studies of neighboring countries.

The comparative administration is an academic effort to extract strategies for building general theories and improving administration by studying the administrative systems and behaviors of various countries. Following the conceptual review of comparative administration theory, the purpose pursued by comparative administration theory is as follows.

First, it is to compare the administrative systems of each country and deduces general characteristics.

Second, it is to explore the administrative features and factors that work differently depending on the country.

Third, it is to verify the cultural, political, and social factors that affect the success or failure of the administrative system.

Fourth, it is to explain the difference in the behaviors of bureaucrats by country and culture.

Fifth, it is to clarify what changes should be induced and how they can be induced to improve the ability of the bureaucracy.

Sixth, it is to establish conceptual knowledge rather than knowledge about detailed facts of each country.

2) The Development Process of Comparative Administration Theory

The development process of the comparative administrative theory is divided into three stages: preparation, prime, and decline.

The first stage is the preparatory period from 1945 to 1962. This period can be regarded as the beginning of the comparative administration. It is the time when the United States took the initiative in the international arena and began providing aid to developing countries after the end of World War II, and the need for comparative administration was raised. However, comparative administrative research has not yet been dealt with in earnest at this time.

The second phase is the heyday, from 1962 to 1971. This period can be defined as from 1962 when the Ford Foundation's support for the Comparative Administration Group, a subcommittee of the

American Society for Public Administration, began, until 1971 when the support was suspended. During this period, the Comparative Administration Group published several papers in collaboration with the Duke University Press, and also published a journal called *Comparative Administration Journal* with Sage. Moreover, the comparative administrative theory was opened and lectured at various universities.

At this time, the Comparative Administration Group led the F. W. Riggs as chairman for over ten years and achieved remarkable growth. As a result, by 1968, membership expanded to reach 500. Besides, the Comparative Administration Group has been conducting various activities to stimulate interest in comparative administration. The initial emphasis was on a series of summer seminars, and in the latter part, they focused on revitalizing research by paying subsidies for experimental educational programs.

The third phase is the decline period, from 1971 onwards. At this time, the Ford Foundation, which has provided considerable support to the Comparative Administration Group, ended its support. Besides, the United States foreign aid has also decreased, and the Comparative Administration Group has become neglected. As a result, comparative administration lectures have been maintained at some universities, but their existence has been considerably weakened, unlike in the past.

The Comparative Administration Group, which has led the comparative administration in this period, has disappeared and has been integrated into the Section on International and Comparative Administration of the American Society for Public Administration.

3) The Approach for Comparative Administrative Research

Comparative administrative research requires a model that allows the comparison of administrative systems across national and social peculiarities of each country and the construction of empirical theories of causal relationships between forces and institutions. There are many theoretical models needed to study comparative administration, and it is not easy to find a uniform theoretical model because each scholar presents different models.

However, considering the changing tendency of theoretical models for comparative administrative research, the most commonly used theoretical models and approaches include the general system approach, the nomothetic approach, and the middle range theory approach. Among the various approaches used in comparative administrative research, the approaches suggested by Fred W. Riggs, Ferrel Heady, and Keith M. Henderson, among others will be briefly explored as follows.

■ The Approach Proposed by Fred W. Riggs

Fred W. Riggs describes the trends in theoretical models and approaches for comparative administrative research as follows.

First, research trends shift from a normative approach to an empirical approach. At this time, the normative approach is to study the method of achieving it on the premise of the ideology or value of the administration, whereas the empirical approach refers to a research trend based on facts without premises of value or ideology.

Second, there is a change in the approach from the idiographic approach to the nomothetic approach. Whereas the idiographic approach focuses on a particular country or specific case, the nomothetic approach refers to the comparative study of the administrative general in various countries.

Third, there is a shift in approach from the non-ecological approach to the ecological approach. While the non-ecological approach focuses on the independent study of administrative systems without considering environmental factors, the ecological approach focuses on the interrelationships between administration and environment.

■ The Approach Proposed by Ferrel Heady

Ferrel Heady holds the following as an approach for comparative administrative research depending on the subject or focus of the study.

First, it is a modified, traditional approach. This approach is similar to the previous parochially oriented approach in the past, but the difference is that the focus of the research shifted to a comparative analysis between administrative systems. Therefore, many kinds of literature related to comparative administration belong to this. In general, it deals with the general themes of public administration such as administrative organization, personnel administration, and financial administration from a comparative point of view, or takes a method of comparing and examining the organization and institutions of western administration narratively.

Second, it is a development-oriented approach. This is a way of studying what the administrative requirements are for achieving the development goals. This approach criticizes traditional comparative administrative research as overly comprehensive, abstract, and synthetic without taking into account social changes, and argues that the development administration should be subject to separate research. It is an approach that is typically emphasized by developmentalists such as Edward W. Weidner and Milton J. Esman.

Third, it is a general system approach. This approach is to attempt cross–cultural and comprehensive theoretical constructs with more attention to the formation of typologies and models for comparative analysis than the modified traditional approaches. Therefore, this approach analyzes and analyzes the overall aspects of administration such as personnel administration, finance administration, and local administration as well as critical environmental factors that affect a specific administration system, from the viewpoint of a system.

Representative examples include F. W. Riggs, which introduced and applied the concept of structural-functional analysis developed by Talcott Parsons and Marion Joseph Levy, Jr., who are classified as sociologists. Besides, John T. Dorsey, who established an information-energy model by equilibrium theory based on input-output system analysis, is also included.

Fourth, it is a middle-range theory approach. This is an approach proposed from the viewpoint that since the general system theory model is too comprehensive and abstract to be supported by empirical data, it would be more useful to narrow down the subject of research and concentrate on research. For example, M. Weber's bureaucracy model is best suited to this middle-range model.

■ The Approach Proposed by Keith M. Henderson

Keith M. Henderson distinguishes the research areas of American public administration as cultural administration, comparative administration and development administration, and classifies the approach of comparative administration into the following five categories.

First, it is a bureaucratic system approach. This approach is primarily to study comparative administration with a focus on bureaucracy and policy. It is because bureaucracy exists not only in all countries in common but also as a systematic concept for the comparative study of various administrative systems. After that, a policy approach was added as interest in policy grew. This approach, unlike conventional practice, places great emphasis on policy formation and function of participation.

Second, it is an input-output system approach. This approach focuses on studying the relationship between citizen demands and support are put into the system, and policy has emerged as output in the system.

Third, it is a component approach. This approach focuses on comparing elements that makeup administration, such as the administrative organization, budget system, administrative committee, and front-line administrative agency in each country. This approach includes the modified traditional approach suggested by F. Heady.

Fourth, it is a development approach. This approach is identical to the development-oriented approach proposed by F. Heady.

Fifth, it is a comparative study approach. This approach is a way to find distinctive differences by comparing organizations such as factories, labor unions, hospitals, and research institutes as well as by comparing bureaucracy and public enterprises in each country.

3.2.3 The Relevance of Comparative Administration Theory

1) The Limitations of Comparative Administration Theory

Comparative administration theory has come to be settled as an academic discipline since it emerged in response to academic demands and practical needs. However, it has faced some practical problems in carrying out comparative studies of administrative phenomena. These problems are common in comparative studies, involving administrative research, especially among countries.

First, it is difficult to define an independent research subject. It is almost impossible to distinguish it clearly from the political system when comparing the administrative systems of various countries. Therefore, it is necessary to admit to some extent that the subject of comparative administration research overlaps with or falls in part with that of comparative political theory.

Especially, as the interest and approach of comparative politics shifted from the institutional and structural center of the past to the functional approach centered on the political process, the possibility of duplication with the comparative administration became even higher. As a result, it is difficult to distinguish the administrative aspect, which is a component of the political system, into an independent research field.

The duplication issue of research subjects is also raised within the public administration. For example, comparative public service system, comparative public enterprise, and comparative organizational theory are one area of personnel administration, financial administration, and organizational theory. Thus, the independent research area of the comparative administrative theory is virtually difficult to be defined and may be regarded as an approach or position in administrative research.

This duplication is not as severe as in the case of comparative politics, but it is clear that it raises the question of whether comparative administration theory can be established as an independent academic field. Therefore the problem is that comparative administration theory is so comprehensive and distracting that no field is not in the scope of comparative administration, as is often expressed as identity crisis because the scope and the theoretical framework have not been established and sufficient empirical research has not been done.

Second, bias is likely to be retrofitted in comparative administrative research. Bias can work at each stage, such as finding a problem, collecting and choosing data, and interpreting the results. The most significant factor that leads to bias is ethnocentrism. In the process of observing and comparing external administrative systems and behaviors, there is a good chance that the bias of the researchers who have grown in the places where the cultural environment and value system are different will affect.

For example, in the field of comparative administration, there is a prejudice against the administrative system of the advanced western countries as an unconditionally developed form. Also, there is a tendency to regard impersonal, universal, and liberal tendencies as unconditionally positive in terms of administrative behavior.

Although what type of administration is desirable should be interpreted in consideration of the cultural tradition and reality of the country, there is a high possibility that the prejudice of researchers will be introduced in international studies. This is an essential issue in the comparative administration that is aiming at value-neutral research.

It is pointed out that there is a lack of scientific and empirical approach in the research method due to criticism raised in this regard. In the case of the underdeveloped countries, it is true that there is not enough data to use and that there are restrictions on the empirical research, but the criticism that the comparative administration is inferior to the other neighboring fields in terms of the research method.

Third, there is the question of what dimension to set the subject of comparative administration. It is doubtful how useful the theory extracted will be if each country is used as a case or sample in the process of attempting empirical verification by setting a hypothesis. Conceptually, even if it is a general theory, if feasibility and practical applicability are low, it is nothing more than a study for research. Therefore, the extent to which the object of comparative research will be extended to the extent that it will be tested is a kind of dilemma in both generalization and practicalization of theory.

Fourth, it is a criticism about the usefulness of research on comparative administration. It is pointed out that pure scholars were in the basis of the composition of the comparative administration group, so it did not deviate from the nature of the ivory tower, and the research results were not very helpful to the administrative scene. Although the concept of development administration has been proposed in order to enhance this relevance, it did not contribute much to solving the actual administrative problems.

2) The Applicability of Comparative Administration Theory

The future of comparative administration theory is not as bright as it once was when it flourished. The large-scale technical assistance was over, and the Comparative Administration Group, which was an active player, was dismantled, and the programs that they started were over or suspended.

Expectations that the comparative administration can contribute to administrative reform in developing countries have also been much lower through comparative administration research, and comparative administration faces much criticism in academia. The comparative administrative research has reduced the expectation that it can contribute to the administrative reform of the developing countries, and the comparative administration faces much criticism in academia.

However, these criticisms are mostly about priorities or methodologies rather than about the necessity of comparative administration or research performance. Comparative administrative research should be activated, but it seems that there is little objection to the reestablishment of its character or approach.

Despite the many criticisms being made on comparative administration theory, comparative administration theory must have made an important contribution to the development of administrative theory.

First, it enlarges the horizon of administrative theory by expanding the domestic administration realm centered on the United States to foreign countries. In other words, it has transformed the subject of research into a new country with different factors and environments from Western-oriented administrative research.

Second, comparative studies with other countries conducted before World War II mainly depended on the institutional approach in terms of research methodology. On the contrary, comparative administrative research has contributed to strengthening the rational and scientific standards for comparison by converting to a relatively functional approach.

Third, the expansion of universality pursued by comparative administrative research has led to significant innovation in the academic atmosphere that has been emphasized before by the peculiarity of administration. It was to seek the construction of administrative theory beyond time and space.

Chapter IV

Public Administration in the Prosperity Period

1. The Story of the Public Administration in the Prosperity Period

In the development of administrative theory, it is not easy to find the period when the atmosphere of the times as much as the 1960s influenced the administration. The administration of the 1960s, when the systems approach was prevailing, was full of conviction in all aspects, including the demands for change and the abilities and skills needed to facilitate change. Thus, Dwight Waldo recalled the 1960s as a period of a scientific and technological climax.

The first political event that took place in the 1950s and 1960s was the inauguration of President John F. Kennedy. He set a national goal in 1961 for an American astronaut to land on the moon by the end of the 1960s, and NASA finally achieved its goal in 1969.

The next president, Lyndon B. Johnson has embodied the Great Society program on an unprecedented scale in terms of social intervention and change. The scope of the social program embodied by the Johnson administration was similar to the New Deal policy. The Johnson administration has begun to simultaneously pursue projects similar to such programs, a series of policies aimed at revitalizing the economy through tax cuts.

The so-called Keynesian-based economic policy has been put in place to allow the government to manage the national economy through financial technologies. As a result, the 1960s seemed to have fewer obstacles that were not overcome by modern administrative states only on the surface. Only proper policy analysis and planning, advanced management systems, new professional and scientific skills, and implementation of administration were required. Thus, in the 1960s, the administration was rapidly expanding, and the administrative theory was also a period of rapid growth and development.

First of all, from the late 1950s, the limit of cultural perquisites and universal validity of American public administration begun to be revealed. Accordingly, comparative administrative research, which emerged to create a typical application of public administration in all areas of the developed and developed countries, became more active in the 1960s. Centered on the Comparative Administration Group led by Fred W. Riggs conducted comparative administrative research in the 1960s. The prismatic sala model attempted by F. W. Riggs to describe the administrative system of developing countries was one of the representative achievements of comparative administrative research.

However, while F. W. Riggs took the ecological approach of John M. Gaus and grasped the administrative behavior of developing countries in the socio-cultural context, it was problematic that he underestimated the uniqueness of the administration and treated it as a dependent variable, overemphasizing the impact of the environment.

In this regard, development administration theory has emerged due to the need to acknowledge the uniqueness of administration and to examine the impact of the administration on the environment. The development administration has mainly focused on dealing with the role of the administration about the development problems of developing countries.

In other words, the purpose of the study was to focus on the administration's role as a means to promote national development, and to present strategies and prescriptions on how to select and manage development projects. Therefore, the development administration has a normative and policy-oriented research character.

Besides, a systematic approach heavily influenced social science in the development of administrative theory in the 1960s. Based on the systematic concept of the 1960s, D. Katz and R. L. Kahn published *The Social Psychology of Organizations* in 1966. In this book, Daniel Katz and Robert Louis Kahn attempted to apply the existing knowledge of the social system, especially in the organization, to the framework of the systems from the systemic viewpoint to help understand the organization's operations.

Meanwhile, planning, programming, budgeting systems(PPBS) dominated the budget of the 1960s. While the planning, programming, budgeting system developed by David Novick in 1968 has been a remarkable success in the Department of Defense and the system has been used so far, internal agencies have raised many questions about their effectiveness. Many states adopted the planning programming budgeting systems, which was introduced as part of a systematic approach in the years to come.

Initially, the planning programming budgeting systems was partially introduced to the Department of Defense in the Kennedy administration, which was evaluated as having increased the rationality of the budget process at the time. As a result, the Johnson administration in 1965 ordered all federal agencies to introduce the planning programming budgeting systems.

All agencies are required to provide detailed descriptions of the purpose and assessment items of the program, to anticipate spending for five years, and to examine cost-benefit analysis and program activities based on zero bases. The application of such planning programming budgeting systems is an example of how the management systems approach has peaked.

In 1966, when the planning programming budgeting systems introduced as part of a systematic approach was on the way to proliferation, Allen Schick published "The Road to PPB: The Stages of Budget Reform" in the *American Public Administration Review*. In this paper, he described the development of budget theory in a chronological way, such as the characteristics of line-item budgeting system taking into account control and responsibility, the performance-based budgeting system emphasizing the effectiveness of management, the planning programming budgeting systems emphasizing goals, planning, and program effectiveness.

In particular, A. Schick inferred the concept and rationality of the planning programming budgeting systems and historically identified how the budget reform has been carried out in this paper. Accordingly, his paper in the field of the public budget has become a milestone, and many scholars have regarded him as a representative figure in studying public budget as a management system approach.

Along with the systematic approach that had a significant influence on the administration in the 1960s, the area where the mutual growth took place was the realm of policy science. In the 1960s, the academic system of management science was completed, such as the introduction of techniques such as operation research and system analysis in the public sector, which promoted administrative reform.

From this point of view, the planning programming budgeting systems introduced in the 1960s was a representative product of administrative reform achievements using the techniques of management science. Also, as the interest in the achievements of the Great Society Programs promoted by the Johnson administration increased, a new trend of policy research began to emerge, resulting in the formation of an academic system called policy science.

The term 'policy sciences' was first used in 1951 by Harold Dwight Lasswell in a paper entitled *Policy Orientation*, but it was in the 1960s that policy studies began to develop in earnest. The focus of early policy science was on the politics of policy-making process and the implementation of specific programs, but by the 1960s, many policy-related academic journals were published, creating an intellectual soil for the growth and development of policy science.

At this point, in particular, the importance of policy analysis was raised by Yehezkel Dror. In 1967, "Policy Analysts: A New Professional Role in Government Service" published in the *American Public Administration Review* played a significant role in invoking new perspectives and the importance of policy analysis.

The systematic approach that affected the realm of budget theory and policy theory did not lag behind its influence in the area of organization and bureaucratic behavior. In 1967, two articles were published that gave a sober analysis of the bureaucracy and put an end to it.

One was Anthony Downs' *Inside Bureaucracy*. In this book, he sought to develop the laws and propositions that help predict the behavior of the American government and bureaucrats through the analysis of American bureaucracy. The other was the paper entitled "Organizations of the Future," published by Warren G. Bennis in 1967 in the *Personnel Administration.*

W. G. Bennis signaled the death of the bureaucracy at a time when society was spreading more and more exchanges with bureaucratic institutions. He predicted that future societies would demand rapid organizational and technological change, participatory management, and the growth of a more specialized labor force, which he criticized for not being able to cope with this future with the current organizational form.

W. G. Bennis emphasized the need for an organization to be reactively and flexibly by pursuing non-bureaucratic and unstructured as an alternative to a future organization. Since then, he has expanded the scope of this thinking and published *The Temporary Society* in 1968, co-authored with Philip E. Slater.

He also tried to predict the effects of new organizational forms while compiling the lessons learned from behavioral science and open-system theory in this paper. The examples he listed were mainly external, with the position that the focus, among other things, should be placed on the impact and interaction of the organization on society. He, in particular, paid keen attention to democratic organizational leadership in this process, which, as it enters the 1980s, develops into a transformational leadership idea.

In conclusion, many peoples regard him as a scholar who has constructed an organizational concept that will come to a different future from the past about human behavior, values, power, and organizational form.

In the 1960s, not only in the academic field but also in the government sector was a time when administrative theories were expanded, and significant changes were brought about. In a nutshell, the Great Society Program, which the Johnson administration attempted, stimulated public officials working in state and local governments, giving them various support and encouragement to achieve their academic growth.

Despite this growth, however, the 1960s was ending with many questions left in many areas. For example, the Vietnam War was the case, and so was the students' militancy formed by it. Also, delicate and sensitive customer groups that have not been seen in the past have begun to emerge, and concepts such as equality of employment opportunity and representative bureaucracy have begun to take effect or emerge.

Dwight Waldo was the scholar who attempted an excellent analysis of the effects of these problems on public administration. He dealt with epochal tides in the "Public Administration in a Time of Revolution," published in 1968 in the *American Public Administration Review*. In this paper, D. Waldo diluted the idea of revolution by questioning whether the 1960s was a substantial period of revolution, instead of by downgrading it into a contemporary revolution. D. Waldo later used the term turbulence instead of the term revolution. In 1971, he published the *Public Administration in a Time of Turbulence.*

However, high expectations for technology and science, bureaucracy, massive government, and society are so realistic that they are calling for a serious and comprehensive response to this. D. Waldo's analysis of the effects of the period of revolution later provided a great stimulus for self-examination.

While the topics raised in D. Waldo's paper - "the content and demands of social equity, expansion of civic engagement and organizational humanism" emerged in the 1960s - have become apparent, there has been a little result of them at this time. As a result, the issues raised by Waldo in the 1970s became the main forum for discussion in the public administration, and attempts to reform the administration was bound to be the main focus.

Meanwhile, social unrest and administrative dissatisfaction caused by the Vietnam War characterized the end of the 1960s. Some management systems and programs developed in the 1960s began to come under criticism, and it was around this time that the planning programming budgeting systems, which was a symbol of the systematic approach, was on the cutting edge.

The first scholar to raise the issue that the value of the planning programming budgeting systems has disappeared was Aron B. Wildavsky. In his book, *The Politics of the Budgetary Process*, published in 1964, Aron Bernard Wildavsky argued that political considerations into an incremental process formed budgets. On the extension of this line, he criticized the planning programming budgeting systems as a useless plan with a scathing criticism of it through the "Rescuing Policy Analysis from PPBS" published in 1969 by the *American Public Administration Review*.

In this paper, A. B. Waldavsky showed how the analytical functions and planning of the planning programming budgeting systems conflict with the essential nature of the budget. As a result, federal agencies and most states and local governments that introduced the planning programming budgeting systems had almost abandoned this system by the end of the 1960s.

Despite this trend, the planning programming budgeting systems still has an impact as a significant budget system, albeit problematic. However, this system still exists in a modified form rather than the planning programming budgeting systems introduced in the early days.

Among the features of the 1960s is the activity of political activists. One of their main slogans was to give back power to the people. In administrative terms, this is called decentralization of public services; of course, the most maximized argument for decentralization was anarchism. Concerning decentralization, Herbert Kaufman published the "Administration Decentralization and Political Power" in 1969 in the *American Public Administration Review*.

H. Kaufman's interest in decentralization has been placed on the issues of leadership, bureaucratic representation, and political neutrality. H. Kaufmann argued that new modes of representation are required to encompass the people in complex modern societies, while at the same time, responsive administration should be established. However, what he implied was something that could not be solved by the administrative capacity of the 1960s. So he instead proposed ways to further strengthen the influence of the region through administrative decentralization at the time of public policy-making.

H. Kaufman also acknowledged that conflicts could arise as a side effect of administrative decentralization. In other words, it may interfere with the pursuit of the national authority to promote economic and social equality, or may result in unproductive competition between local governments and programs, or cause inefficiency in government operations. Nevertheless, he thought that the best alternative was administrative decentralization in the context of the situation.

The last voice that embellished the 1960s, a time of significant change, came from Theodore Jay Lowi. In his 1969 edition of *The End of Liberalism: Ideology, Policy and the Crisis of Public Authority*, he lashed out at the harsh criticism of the democratic government, as well as the crippling the American policy process due to pluralism based on interest groups. However, T. J. Lowi criticism is discriminatory in that it shows a counter-argument to the decentralization that H. Kaufman claimed.

Finally, the development of the government reforms in the 1960s, especially the civil rights movement and poverty eradication projects, has evoked interest in the impact of the administration on individuals. In this context, the new public administration movement emerged.

In September 1968, under the auspices of Dwight Waldo, young scholars and practitioners gathered in Minnowbrook to hold a conference, where they emphasized the independent identity of public administration based on relevance, participation, change, values, and social equity.

The new public administration movement demanded policy-oriented administration to restore the practical nature and relevance of public administration. Moreover, it criticized the obsession with professionalism and value-neutral management theory, emphasizing decentralization, client control, and consensus on values based on democratic value norms. Besides, the new public administration movement emphasized the active role of the administrator, claiming that the administration should provide quality services for the political, economic, and social disadvantaged, and realize social equality.

The new public administration, in this way, eschewed the efficiency-directed pursued by the orthodox administration and advocated social equality, democratic value, proactive administration based on humanism, and customer-oriented administration. To this end, the new public administration proposed debureaucratic organizational design as an alternative, criticized logical positivism and behavioralism, and presented a phenomenological approach.

In the end, the new public administration emphasized norm-oriented rather than value-neutral, prescriptive rather than descriptive, customer-oriented rather than institution-oriented. The intellectual tradition of the new public administration has since been in line with the critical public administration or the action theory, which emerged around the 1980s.

Meanwhile, the second Minnowbrook conference was held in 1988, 20 years after the first Minnowbrook conference was convened. At the conference, unlike the past, the behavioral science has been highly appreciated for its contributions to the development of public administration, and the issues such as public officials' ethics, social equality, human relations theory, and harmony of administration and democracy were discussed as new agenda.

In conclusion, the 1960s, when it was a time of great promise and change, gave new resistance and limitations to administration both internally and externally. As a result, the new public administration movement formed the agenda for self-reflection of the administration and reform, and this subject was bound to become the most critical issue in the 1970s.

2. The Representative Scholars in the Prosperity Period

The characteristics of the developmental process of the 1960s administrative theory characterized by the period of such a profound change are as follows from the standpoint of representative scholars.

2.1 Fred W. Riggs's Prismatic Model

According to Fred W. Riggs, two kinds of knowledge are needed to study administrative reform or administrative development with normative theory. One should have explicit knowledge of the relationship between the administrative situation and administrative history, and the other should be able to make the causal relationship between administrative variables a verifiable hypothesis.

In this respect, the model that has been used in public administration and politics is the result of studying European countries such as the United States and the United Kingdom. In other words, these countries have relatively similar environmental factors, meaning that they have studied administrative systems or administrative entities by considering them as being independent, ignoring the environment or background.

However, if the administration of non-European countries is studied as a non-ecological model with the hypothesis of institutional autonomy, or if the principle is derived from this model and applied to develop countries, the model or theory will inevitably become useless.

So in order not to result in such a result, it is necessary to create a model with an ecological base that can help study remote administration. In this case, there was a problem with the fact that even making a model would be challenging to find the relevance of the model in the study of developing countries, which are a mixture of traditional factors and industrial modernization.

The starting point of the discussion of F. W. Riggs began with the development of an analytical model suitable for studying a developing country, the third type of state, not a traditionally agricultural country with traditional elements or not industrial country that has been modernized. Accordingly, F. W. Riggs proposed a prismatic model as a model for analyzing developing countries with characteristics of transitional societies.

The term 'prismatic' is a concept borrowed from structural-functional analysis, which means a part of an extensive system. Therefore, the prismatic model can be considered the intermediate type of a fused society model that helps study traditional and backward societies and a refracted societies model that is useful for analyzing advanced Western industrial societies. In other words, a prismatic model was set up to explain the characteristics of the transitional society that remains in the middle stage between an agricultural society and an industrial society.

In prismatic societies, due to the diversity of its structure, sub-models such as politics, administration, society, economy, and religion can be created. At this time, the Sala model was created to explain the administrative sub-model of prismatic society.

In other words, Sala means an administrative submodel in a prismatic society. In Asia, Sala is also used as an office, but it is also used as a place for pavilion, drawing room, or religious gatherings. So in a refracted society, similar forms to Sala are office or bureau. However, Sala has a different meaning from home or court, that means a place in a fused traditional society.

2.1.1 The Characteristics of Prismatic Society

As a model for analyzing the characteristics of developing countries, the characteristics of prismatic society proposed by F. W. Riggs are as follows.

First, a high degree of heterogeneity is a characteristic of a prismatic society. Heterogeneity refers to a state in which traditional and fused characteristics and modern and refracted characteristics are mixed extensively. As a result, the most prominent administrative feature of the prismatic society can be found in the Sala model. For example, in the prismatic society, the Sala system is a mixture of the bureau of modern meaning or the court in the traditional sense.

Second, a high degree of formalism is a characteristic of prismatic society. Formalism is a difference between the official norm and its actual application, which means the degree of difference or inconsistency between institution and practice. The most prominent feature of the Sala model itself is that formalism is seriously rampant.

In other words, it is an example that the law and the actual behavior of the bureaucrat operate entirely separately. The increased administrative discretion of bureaucrats characterized the

Sala model, primarily due to the deepening of formalism, which in turn is likely to lead to cronyism or corruption.

Third, overlapping is a characteristic of prismatic society. Overlapping means that the specialized structures of differentiated societies coexist with the unspecialized structures of convergent societies. In prismatic societies, for example, new institutions such as the government, parliament, electoral systems, schools are introduced, while those such as administration, politics, economy, and education are continuously carried out by an undifferentiated structure: family, religious group, or particular class or faction.

As a result, while a new norm or value system suitable for a differentiated structure are only treated outwardly, the old values of traditional and unspecialized society persist strongly. Thus, overlapping results in social schizophrenia between conscious public forms and informal unconscious behaviors.

Fourth, the characteristics of the prismatic society include poly-communalism and clects. In a prismatic society, many communities are bound by realities such as regionalism, school relations, and blood relationship, and the phenomenon of multiple factionalism in which confrontations and struggles are severe is widespread.

A modern organizational form has these characteristics on the surface, but it has a factional character that only blind loyalty is forced. As a result, the formation of faction in the Salah system will inevitably hinder the formation of a universal norm of government or public offices in a differentiated society. In other words, it is highly likely that the overlapping is contradictory to the regulatory norms of the Sala system.

Fifth, the prismatic society is characterized by the uncertainty of the price, which is characteristic of the bazaar-canteen model. The bazaar-canteen model is a submodel of the prismatic society. This bazaar-canteen means a society in which the price of goods is fixed, but the actual transaction price depends on environmental factors, such as the bond between sellers and buyers, or negotiation power or power.

As a result, under the Sala system dominated by the bazaar canteen model, price indeterminacy is involved wherever money is attached, such as salaries, purchases, contracts, fringe income, accounting inspections.

Sixth, the characteristics of the prismatic society include poly-normativism and a lack of consensus. The government offices of the differentiated society presuppose the basic principles or axioms that all the participants, the customers who are the object of control and service, as well as the management of the government, can understand.

On the other hand, these conditions do not exist in prismatic society. In other words, as norms or myths based on traditional societies still influence, they lack essential consensus. Poly- normativism appears in a severe form in the Sala system. For example, management seems to adhere to the publicly objective and achievement-oriented recruitment standards, the equality of status and universal norms, but in reality, it is subject to subjective, identity standards, rigid class, and exclusive norms.

2.1.2 The Limitations of Model

The prismatic model proposed by F. W. Riggs to explain the

characteristics of developing countries and the Sala system, which is a model for describing the sub-administrative system of such societies, contributed significantly to the development of comparative administration research. Nevertheless, this model has problems in some ways.

First, the model itself is a balance theory based on structural-functional analysis and has not been able to deal with social changes because of its static nature adequately. Accordingly, there is a considerable problem in that the administration is regarded as a passive being of the environment from a deterministic point of view or in terms of its negligence in the fact that creative elites can change the environment.

In particular, if new ideas and systems are introduced, the potential of developing countries is underestimated by overlooking the possibility of leading them to development.

Second, it is a matter of whether the characteristics of the prismatic society, which F. W. Riggs means, are indeed pathologic factors. Rational thinking in the West is the basis of the criteria proposed by F. W. Riggs, but not necessarily in terms of developing countries.

The standards that F. W. Riggs proposes are based on rational thinking in the West, and in the situation of developing countries, it can not be said to be pathologic. This phenomenon is often found in industrial societies, and this model faces criticism as a model based on cultural superiority.

2.2 Daniel Katz and Robert Louis Kahn's Social Psychology of Organization

Daniel Katz and Robert Louis Kahn attempted to apply the social system perspective to the organization. In other words, it is significant in terms of presenting the framework of the system from a systematic point of view. D. Katz and R. L. Kahn tried to define the nature of the environment by dealing with the problem of how the external environment influences the organization from a systematic viewpoint.

Their research begins with the proposition that the environment is the essential variable in explaining the organizational change. According to D. Katz and R. L. Kahn, the change in the organization is not caused by horizontal and vertical pressure inside the organization, but by input applied outside the organization. Under this pressure, the organization will establish a strategy, in which uncertain environments create a broader and more diverse strategy, and structural changes are triggered to support this strategy.

It is necessary to understand the concept of decision points in order to understand D. Katz and R. L. Kahn's view. As the organization responds to the environmental demand at the decision points, observing these decision points will reveal the adaptation state. There are four types of decision points.

The first is the domain, which determines which of the particular areas to choose and how to develop a strategy for it; the second is the decision to adopt the appropriate technology to enforce the strategy.; the third is the decision to establish structures to control strategies and technologies; and the fourth is the decision to ensure the continuity of the organization.

However, this decision is influenced by top management, but the environment and the decisions already made constrain it. As described above, D. Katz and R. L. Kahn do not care about the closed system or the traditional bureaucratic structure if the organization is stable or controllable through the characterization of the open system. However, if the organizational environment becomes more dynamic and unstable, there is a problem with the survival of the organization.

In conclusion, D. Katz and R. L. Kahn argued that the traditional and closed system view of the organization failed because they failed to correctly recognize the interdependence and interactions between the organization and the environment and that the system theory should be applied to the organizational theory.

2.3 Allen Schick's Budget Reform

Allen Schick is a leading figure in the study of public budgets from a systematic perspective that prevailed in the 1960s. He approached the public budget with a management system approach in 1966 on "The Road to PPB: The Stages of Budget Reform" and in 1969 on "Systems Politics and Systems Budgeting" published in the *American Public Administration Review*.

A. Schick listed the three primary functions of the budget: control management, and planning. He considered three functions as essential norms for designing and operating budget systems. The three functions of control, control, and planning, as the three functions of the budget, were seen as the norms for designing and operating the budget system.

A. Schick explained the development stages of the budget system, focusing on the three main functions of the budget. That is to say, all budget systems, no matter what budget system, contain these functions, but there is a difference in that they emphasize specific functions depending on the type of budget system. For example, there is a difference in that the budget system for line-item budgeting system emphasizes the control function, the performance-based budgeting system for the management function, and the planning programming budgeting systems for the planning function.

In explaining the development process of the budget system, he inferred the concept and rationality of the planning programming budgeting systems from a discriminatory point of view. In particular, his paper in the field of public budgets has become a milestone, historically identifying how a budget reform has been achieved through the development of the budget system.

In addition to identifying the development process of the budget system, the contribution of A. Schick's budget theory is that it approached the budget system from a systematic point of view in the 1960s. He published the above paper to evaluate the first anniversary of the introduction of the planning programming budgeting systems in 1969, in which he stressed that in order for the planning programming budgeting system to succeed, politics and budget system must be reformed anew from a systematic point of view.

In other words, he pointed out the shortcomings of the American political process in the mid-1960s and insisted that politics and budget management should be reformed from a systematic point of view, in the sense that the planning programming budgeting systems helps to make up for them. To this end, he criticized the incrementalism and pluralism that dominate American society and emphasized that it should overcome limitations of conventional process politics and process budget management from a systematic point of view.

Through the introduction of the planning programming budgeting systems based on a systematic perspective, his views on the consideration of the socially and economically weak, the rational allocation of resources and the effectiveness of allocating resources have considerable validity.

However, despite this plausibility, A. Schick's argument has the following problems.

First, it is the overconfidence of elitism. Although it is a limitation of the system theory, the systematic budget management, which sets the goals of the institution from the systematic point of view and determines its policies accordingly, is prone to emphasize centralization. Under this view, the budget is likely to be swayed by a few top decision-makers in charge of the agency's operations.

Second, he criticized pluralism and incrementalism for emphasizing the systematic budget management method, which was heavily dependent on public choice theory and political economics. The theoretical concept upon which he relied was a failure of the market, but there is a problem that the opposition to the market's failure is formidable.

For example, there are risks such as power abuse, corruption, formalism, and rigidity caused when political institutions and bureaucracy replace what invisible hands should do. In other words, there is a problem in that the arbitrary nature of power and the expediency of bureaucracy can lead to inefficiency in the allocation of resources and distort social equity.

2.4 Yehezkel Dror's Revolution of Policy Sciences

Along with the systematic approach that has had a profound impact on administration in the 1960s, the part where the mutual growth took place in the area of policy analysis. Yehezkel Dror emphasized the importance of policy analysis. In his 1967 paper, "Policy Analysts: A New Professional Role in Government Service," published in the *American Public Administration Review*, he evoked the importance of policy analysis.

Despite Harold Dwight Lasswell already advocated the need for policy sciences in 1951, academic progress and interest in it were unsatisfactory, but the scholar who attempted to revive it was Y. Dror. Y. Dror attempted to revive policy sciences by introducing policy analysis as one of the oldest functions in government functions and as a new profession with professionalism. Thus, Y. Dror defined policy analysis as encompassing both policy formation process and policy content.

Y. Dror acknowledges that economic analysis plays a pivotal role in policy analysis, but recognizes that there is a limit to the circumstances in which economics unilaterally determined policy. He also criticized the incremental approach in policy making and was one of the researchers who established the policy sciences approach in which the economic role and the political role should be balanced in policy analysis.

2.4.1 Y. Dror's Revolution of Policy Sciences

Y. Dror argued that policy sciences should include a combination of value-oriented applied research and fact-oriented pure research to improve policy decisions, and even policy sciences should include a superrational and irrational process in the study. To this end, Y. Dror argued that all the scientific theories of the time, such as general system theory, system analysis theory, game theory, cybernetics, and system engineering, should be mobilized to build integrated social sciences.

The reason that Y. Dror has come to emphasize the policy sciences approach was because he believes that policy sciences have yet to reach a mature stage. So he holds the reasons why the scientific revolution is needed in policy sciences as follows.

First, it is an inherent barrier to science. This barrier is due to the conservatism that causes intense backlash when new changes occur in existing theories or models.

Second, it is an obstacle caused by practitioners engaged in the policy-making process. This obstacle is caused by differences in perception of the role in the policymaking process, which stems from a conventional notion that policy-makers can only make policy decisions. Therefore, the area of policy sciences should not merely stay in the process of preparing data for policymakers to refer to but should be involved in all areas that strengthen the democratic political system from the way policymakers decide policies.

After all, due to these obstacles to policy sciences, the development of policy sciences is restricted, which is the necessity of the scientific revolution proposed by Y. Dror.

2.4.2 Y. Dror's Optimal Model

Y. Dror proposed an optimal model as an alternative, given that both rational and incremental models have weaknesses. The optimal model he proposed emphasized the need to utilize human intuition or insight actively. Thus Y. Dror embodied a policy process based on an optimal model. He has divided the policy process into three phases: a meta-policymaking stage, a policymaking stage, and a post-policymaking stage. Moreover, he then subdivided it into 18 stages again.

The first step is the critical policy decision-making stage, which is particularly essential for optimal policy-making. The main contents included in the first phase include ① policy issues, values related to the problems, and available resources are identified and secured, ② design, evaluation, and redesign of the policy decision system, ③ the decision on the policy decision strategy.

The second step is the policy decision-making phase, which is generally similar to the policy-making stage discussed by scholars. This step involves the detailed allocation of resources, the value-determination, and prioritization associated with specific goals, and the best alternative selection.

The third step is the post-policy decision-making phase, where policy implementation takes place. This phase includes the communication and feedback functions that link all phases.

Y. Dror's policy process steps can be highly appreciated in that they are dense in content, as discussed above, and present vital aspects such as the basic policy or the decision-making stage of the basic policy. However, despite the positive aspects, the drawbacks of the process theory are as follows.

First, the decision of the basic policy is not fundamentally different from the original detailed policy decision, and only the abstraction is different depending on its impact and scope. Therefore, the policy decision is refluxed continuously between the decision of the basic direction and the specific decision.

Second, the complexity of the explanation, as seen in the basic policy decision-making, requires more research and work than anything else.

Third, there is no discussion of the policy agenda-setting.

2.5 Aron B. Wildavsky's Politics of the Budgetary Process

Aron Bernard Wildavsky, who was greatly influenced by Charles Edward Lindblom, wrote many books on the budgeting process and fiscal policy. He was interested in the budgeting process, power, and culture, and he paid particular attention to the budget process. He tried to put political process theory under the rule that governs the decision-making process on the budget and to verify it in practice. As a result, he concluded that the budgeting process, the budget system, and the budget preparation all implied political character.

This idea of A. B. Wildavsky's budgeting process is well documented in his masterpiece, *The Politics of the Budgetary*

Process, published in 1964. It is the politics of budgeting process theory that is at the core of A. B. Wildavski's budget theory. In other words, the government's spending decision is not made based on a comprehensive analysis of all alternatives, but rather on the fact that those who participate in the budgeting process pursue only small changes in the political process based on their experiences and past budgets.

This behavior of the participants in the politics of the budgetary process is called an incremental calculation, which is closely related to Herbert A. Simon's bounded rationality, which presupposes the limited calculation capabilities of humans.

For example, in budget managers who have to act within the scope of bounded rationality, budget decisions are bound to be made according to minimal, limited computational ability. As a result, the government's budget decisions are based on an existing budget called a zero-base, which means an ordinary expectation level of budget participants that allocation of budgets will be very close to their existing expenditure levels. In this process, each budget participant has a fair share of the budget allocation, which will ensure robust stability and coordination in the budget process.

The politics of the budgetary process, which A. B. Wildavsky means, is the process of identifying what the government should do in response to the needs of the people and dividing them into areas that can be dealt with within the scope of human bounded rationality. So budget participants reach a consensus on the level of expenditure in different roles and strategies.

In this case, a role is a budget behavior that is expected to be different according to the location of the budget participants, which means a kind of division of labor in budget decisions. A strategy is a form in which budget participants exert influence on the budget decision process according to different roles.

In the end, if politics is a decision about who has what, then budget politics is a decision about who gets what the government has to give. Thus, the expression of political conflicts according to different preferences of the people is an essential aspect of budget research. In this way, A. B. Wildavsky enumerated wealth, prediction of financial resources, and political culture, including the political system as environmental variables that affect the political decision-making process of the budget. Besides, he also observed that wealth and prediction among these variables are particularly important in determining the budget pattern.

Meanwhile, the incrementalism and politics of the budgetary process proposed by A. B. Wildavsky have the following problems despite the advantages of the analysis. For example, the budget system for the line-item budgeting system, the performance-based budgeting system, the planning programming budgeting systems, the zero-based budget system, and the target budget system are all budget systems that seek rationality. That is to say; these systems are based on the premise of closeness to the environment in the budget process.

On the other hand, the incremental budget is to pursue politics in the budget process and emphasizes the political process with the environment surrounding the budget process. Accordingly, the incremental budget can minimize conflicts and resolve the instability of the project.

Also, incremental budgets can minimize the likelihood that

projects that must be provided for equity but that may be eliminated because of inefficiency, such as the budget for welfare services that subsidize the poor, will disappear from the budget process. So the best environment for the incremental budget to be applied is in a society dominated by economic growth or pluralism like the 1960s.

However, incremental budgets are very complicated to use when government finances are severe, such as during the economic downturn. The incremental budget model also implies the limitation of the difficulty of using it in a place where the environment surrounding the budget process has changed drastically since the 1980s, such as the welfare state and the difficulty in taxation on capital.

2.6 Theodore Jay Lowi's End of Liberalism and Policy Typology

In the development of administrative theory, Theodore Jay Lowi's contribution can be divided into two aspects: the diagnosis of the pathology of American democracy and the role of policy scholars.

2.6.1 T. J. Lowi's End of Liberalism

The final voice to decorate the 1960s, a period of immense change, came from T. J. Lowi. He preached that democracy in the United States could only be protected if pluralistic incrementalism and the liberal philosophy based on interest groups, which are the ideological foundations of the political and administrative process dominating the United States were to be fundamentally dismissed.

His ideas were embodied in his 1969 publication of *The End of Liberalism: Ideology, Policy, and the Crisis of Public Authority*. In this book, T. J. Lowi harshly criticized the democratic government, as well as the crippling of the American policy process due to the pluralism based on interest groups.

In other words, T. J. Lowi argued that the passage of its public authority into the hands of interest groups has weakened the government's public authority and that its pursuit of decentralized government has put the government in a difficult situation, with the central government unable to formulate long-term plans.

That is to say; he pointed out that the interest groups that took control of mighty powers had a great interest in maximizing their interests, but that the problem was dangerous because they did not show any interest in promoting the public interest. So T. J. Lowi considered the entire government activity based on pluralistic incrementalism as corruption.

In the end, he diagnosed that the liberalism in the United States was reduced to liberalism centered on interest groups, losing true freedom and that genuine civic participation and sound democratic politics began to take a path of corruption due to the liberalism centered on interest groups. In this respect, his view is at odds with the decentralization emphasized by Herbert Kaufman.

He saw that the profit-oriented liberalism that dominates American society has made it impossible for the government, which has been in charge of difficult choices among conflicting values, to function anymore.

T. J. Lowi cited various interests being created through alliances among interest groups, relevant government agencies, and committees of the legislature, and passed through interactions between them because the government could no longer perform conflict mediation functions. So he took a critical stance that the regulatory agency protected the regulatory group, refusing the advantages of the pluralistic interest group theory that group theorists claim.

Many scholars widely accepted his critical analysis of the American government as accurate and sharp, but his prescription for returning to legal or constitutional democracy, which is equivalent to the juridical democracy he suggested as an alternative, seems problematic.

In conclusion, many scholars have evaluated T. J. Lowi's work on the American government as a meaningful study that accurately extracts the features of the American government in the 1960s. The 1976 issue of the "American Government: The Incomplete Conquest" illustrated T. J. Lowi's ideas.

2.6.2 T. J. Lowi's Policy Typology

T. J. Lowi was a scholar who advocated the need for a new methodological change in policy research from the point of integrating pluralism and elitism. He raised this need in a 1964 edition of the "American Business, Public Policy, Case Studies, and Political Theory." In this paper, T. J. Lowi tried to reveal how various policy problems arise from different types of policies, and also to analyze the impact and intensity of different policy types on the policy process.

Due to his research, policy research has shifted from a process-oriented micro discussion to a macroscopic perspective, and as a result, the contents of policy actions have been treated as independent variables to study policy phenomena. In other words, he emphasized the necessity of comparative studies and case analysis of more new policies and opened a new horizon of analytical perspective.

Besides being the first full-fledged study of policy typology, his policy type theory is monumental in that it offers a proposition that policies affect the political process, breaking away from the popular myth that policies are the product of the political process.

According to T. J. Lowi, the type of policy involved determines political relations, and therefore, a unique type of political relationship is formed according to each policy. This is because their expectation determines the type of relationship between political participants, and the policy governs the expectation as a government output. At this time, the political relationship can be seen as a power relationship or a power structure in the long run. Thus, the proposition that policy types determine political relations implies that the power structure varies with the type of policy.

In other words, for T. J. Lowi, the arena of policy means the arena of power at the same time. This meaning can be easily understood by considering his fundamental proposition that policy determines political relations. In other words, depending on the policy type, a unique political structure, political process, and interaction patterns between elites and groups develop.

Finally, T. J. Lowi distinguished the policy type as distributive policy, regulatory policy, redistributive policy, and compositive policy based on the effect or influence of policy on society.

However, his policy typology generally has limitations in escaping the problems of typology.

As a problem that can be pointed out as a limit, the ground theory that provides clear criteria for policy typing is weak, and the category of policy type is not mutually exclusive. So, it is pointed out that it is difficult to verify empirically, and especially in the case of regulatory policy, the category is not clear. As a limit to the ground theory, which gives clear criteria for policy typification as a problem that can be pointed out, is weak and the category of policy type is virtually not mutually exclusive. Besides, it is difficult to verify empirically, especially in the case of regulatory policy, the category is not clear.

In conclusion, his policy typology may be meaningful in that it presents an essential precursor for policy research despite its limitations.

3. The Representative Theory in the Prosperity Period

The representative administrative theories that emerged in the prosperity period of public administration are system theory and new public administration theory. The background, characteristics, and contents of the theories that led to the formation of these theories are as follows.

In the case of system theory, however, the general system theory must be the core content in system theory. However, it is necessary to explain separately the political system theory influenced by the general system theory because it is necessary to look separately at the impact of political system theory on administrative studies, as well as the volume of describing these two at once.

3.1 General System Theory

3.1.1 The Background of General System Theory

General system theory or general systems approach originated from two similar schools outside of political studies, namely sociological functionalism, and general systems theory.

1) Functionalism as the Mother of System Theory

Functionalism, which forms the mainstream of American sociology, has maintained its position in favor of holistic tradition in terms of sociological thought. The holistic theory is a view that gives an analytical superiority to a larger entity that can not be explained at all in terms of individual behavior and interaction. From this tradition, functional sociology was the result of the evolution of early organicism in that it focused on problems in the whole society and derived explanatory concepts through analogy from biological organicism.

Functional sociology has thus transformed the ideas of society into a social system. So, in functional sociology, the key term for analysis is structure and function. At this time, structure refers to patterns of action in the social system and can be regarded as generalization with the basis of direct experience.

The function, on the other hand, is a term that implies complexity. The concept of function is widely used, but the precise definition is a controversial issue. The function is not just a specific set of things that can be observed. It is in a broader sense to understand specific activities or their relation to the system as a whole. Therefore, the concept of function implies the meaning of discriminating the given activity effect on the continuation of the system, which is more complicated than simple empirical generalization.

Political scientists have also used the functional approach developed in sociology. The functions of social systems, ancillary structures, and structures raised by sociologists to maintain the system have had a profound influence on the political system research of political scientists. As a prominent scholar, Gabriel A. Almond, he applied a structural and functional approach to political science.

2) The General System Theory as the Mother of System Theory

General system theory has evolved from biology and emerged as part of an academic movement aimed at unification of science and scientific analysis. Ludwig von Bertalanffy founded general system theory in 1920 and developed after the World War Ⅱ. The main reason for the emergence of the general system theory was to avoid unnecessary, redundant research as the studies were not only closed but also blocked from interdisciplinary exchanges. Thus, The search for the direction of the integration of science was finally realized in 1949.

Scholars in a variety of disciplines have organized the Committee on Behavioral Sciences at the University of Chicago, allowing them to attempt to establish a general theory that provides empirical verification of behavior. Meanwhile, the Committee on Behavioral Sciences published the *Design for a Brain* in 1952 and *An Introduction to Cybernetics* in 1956. In 1956, the Society for the Advance of General Systems Research was organized and published. Also, in the same year, *Toward a Unified Theory of Human Behavior*, edited by Roy Richard Grinker, was published.

As a result, general system theory has had a significant impact on adjacent science and academia. After all, general system theory is a model of the general aspect of reality as a way of looking at things that were previously overlooked. In this sense, general system theory is a methodological lesson that is related to the permanent problem of philosophy and can also be seen as an effort to answer this question.

3.1.2 The Contents and Characteristics of General System Theory

1) The Significance of General System Theory

At the end of World War Ⅱ, the need to construct a set of systematic theories to discuss the general relationships of the empirical world began to be emphasized in each academic and scientific field. As a result, these fruits emerged as an exploration of general system theory. However, constructing a systematic theory does not mean that it is intended to replace the special theory of a particular discipline with a single, self-sufficient general theory.

Practically speaking, we mention everything means there is almost nothing. However, at each level of abstraction, there must be an optimum degree of generality between a particular thing with no meaning and a generic one without content. Thus the core of the general system theory is based on the assumption that, in theory, a particular science cannot reach optimality.

The purpose of the general system theory was to be established based on ambition and conviction. Based on a high level of conviction and low-level ambition, similarities are extracted for the abstract composition of different disciplines, and to develop a theoretical model that could be applied in at least two different areas.

This was an attempt to develop something like a system of systems that will function as a gestalt in a theoretical configuration, based on a low level of confidence and high-level ambition. As in the definition of economist Kenneth Ewart Bowling, it is common to regard general system theory as a name used to describe the level of theoretical model establishment in intermediate positions, between the generalized composition of mathematics and the particular theory of the specialized discipline.

2) The Goals and Assumptions of General System Theory

The general system theory aims to pursue the universal principles of the systems covered in each discipline. Therefore, the general system theory tends to pursue the following tendencies or pursue smaller goals.

First, there is a general tendency to pursue integration in the fields of natural and social sciences.

Second, this integration tends to focus on the general theory of the system.

Third, the field of nonmaterial science can be an essential means of developing accurate theories.

Fourth, the general system theory seeks to approach the goal of the unification of science by developing an integrated principle that can bind individual science together.

Fifth, as a result, general system theory can pursue the integration requested in science education.

The reason why general system theory sets such a goal is that it has the following assumptions.

First, the central notion of general system theory begins with the idea that organized complexity arises from primitive disorder. This idea is the most critical aspect of general system theory in the sense that the chemical creation of the universe, the origin of life, or social evolution is like this. In this sense, the fundamental problem of science today has evolved into an idea of organized complexity. According to this idea, traditional physics deals with organization, holism, direction, teleology, and differentiation.

Second, the various characteristics of the system that bring about the organized complexity are similar in different areas. Because of the common characteristics of the system, structural similarity, or structural homogeneity can be found in different fields. Structural homogeneity provides similar concepts, models, and laws developed in specific fields, and the possibility of applying them in other fields.

3) The Main Concept of General System Theory

The components that make up the general system theory are very complex. In particular, since the concepts used in general system theory are closely related to each other, one concept can be understood only about other concepts related to it. In this section, we will look at the basic concepts of these components in order to help them understand the general system theory.

■ System

Defining a system is a set of elements with interrelations. In other words, the system consists of a series of interacting components or elements and has a boundary with attributes that filter inputs from other systems and outputs that flow into other systems.

■ Open System

The assumption of the open system was formulated based on physical and physiological concepts. The open system is a system that exchanges materials with the environment, which forms or disassembles components of material on behalf of its function of input and output of the material.

The opposition of the open system is a closed system, which is isolated from the environment, which increases entropy and eventually stops the process. The entropy is a probability value, but the closed system tends to go into the most probable distribution state.

■ Components

The component is a unit of a system that combines, separates or compares inputs to produce an output with other units.

■ Boundary

The boundary is an area that separates one system from another.

The presence or absence of a boundary is identified by differences between the components when the relationship is within and outside the boundary, which is related to revealing what the relationship is in the basic definition of a system.

That is to say, the boundary of the system is the area in which a change occurs in the characteristics of the interrelationship between elements. Boundaries have attributes of encoding and decoding, so so what is imposed on the system does not immediately enter the system.

In other words, the boundary is a door that determines what to accept within the system and what to send out of the system and controls the flow rate of input and output. Thus, the boundary is the area through which inputs and outputs pass, through which exchange occurs between the system and the environment. The boundary here does not only refer to physical compartments but also includes psychological properties such as norms.

■ State of the System

The components of the system can be thought of as being arranged in a specified pattern at a given time, which is the state of a system. The state of the system may be different at each point in time.

■ Input

Inputs into the system refer to information that has been introduced into the system's energy or system. In this case, the input of energy or information can be divided into maintenance inputs and signal inputs. Among these, the maintenance inputs help to activate the system and enable the operation, and the signal inputs function to provide the system with information to be processed.

In the absence or inadequacy of maintenance or support inputs to the system, the system will be destroyed or damaged, which is crucial in its ability to handle signal inputs and demand inputs.

■ Output

The outputs of the system mean the energy, information, or products that the components of the system send out of the system to the higher systems. There are two types of outputs, one that is useful to the higher system and one that is useless. The distinction of outputs is crucial because they can survive together only when the subsystem provides useful input to the higher system.

However, the input that the system can accept is limited and not indiscriminate. If the useful output is more excellent than useless output, the system and higher systems can grow and survive. Otherwise, the system and the higher system will be dismantled.

■ Feedback

Feedback refers to the control of input as a function of output. The reason why the concept of feedback is vital because it is necessary to use this concept to understand the survival, function, and purpose orientation of the system. The characteristics of the system with feedback can automatically compensate for obstacles that are not known in advance. It is sufficient to know the expected range of interference and the expected extreme values to design such a feedback control system.

The feedback has negative feedback and positive feedback. In negative feedback, when the output reaches the extreme, the information is transmitted, and the level of the input is reduced, and the system is maintained in a stable state through the negative feedback. The positive feedback is the opposite case, which means that the information that the output is less than the extreme value increases the input.

■ Storage and Memory

The system requires a minimum reaction time to convert the input into the output. Storage is a property of the system that can delay the outputs beyond the minimum response time. Storage does not occur in all systems. However, the system that is configured to be storable is more suitable for survival.

The reason for the storage is that first, more input is made than the system needs, and secondly, structural modifications occur in the process of processing the inputs. The energy stored in this way affects the subsequent input process. Also, memory is the storage of signal input.

■ Adaptation

Adaptation of the system is related to variability. In this sense, the output of an open system is probabilistic. Because open systems interact with other systems and other systems are variable, one-to-one correspondence cannot always be established in the connection of inputs and outputs. It is also very uncertain which state the components of the system will produce.

However, the variability of the system is not infinite. The variability of the system output is controlled by the structure and boundaries of the components of the system and is also regulated by the number of system states. Moreover, the capacity of the system is the scope of variability. The higher the extent of variability, the greater the capacity of the system, and the capacity of the system is constrained by the variability constrained.

An organization that appears between components of a system (or between systems) is initially formed when two or more elements accidentally form a symbiotic relationship, and a feedback relationship arises between complex systems. As a result, the organization of the system becomes more complex and has emergent characteristics. The new characteristics are features that can not be found in one level of a system and can also be seen as evolution as features that appear in other levels of a system.

As such, adaptations are made to increase the viability of a system by modifying its behavior and structure amid the variability of the system's output and the complexity, uncertainty, and new characteristics of the system. Eventually, the system adapts by preventing, dispersing, or neutralizing, potentially harmful inputs.

■ Growth of Systems

The growth of systems refers to the expansion of the system scale in which all parts are functionally developed. Growth is structural change, and heterogeneous input causes structural change. In other words, growth begins when a different input is made at a critical point in time, which makes the system in a semi-organized state-organized.

In this respect, the original idea, core, element, or unique material that leads to the growth of the system is different from the inputs which maintain the system or direct the system to work. Due to growth and subsequent modifications, the system has emergent characteristics. Moreover, because growth-based modifications allow the system to remain more efficient, growth-based modifications can be seen as adaptations.

However, there is also a limit to growth, which is constrained by adaptive limits and memory. Also, growth is achieved by the initial plan contained in the substructure of the system. Of course, this plan is modified following the partial specialization, but the initial plan leaves a big trail behind. Learning can be said to be a modification of the structure that occurs due to the input of signals. If there is no change after receiving much information, nothing has been learned.

With growth, there is a new relationship between the subsystem and the upper system, which is created from the subsystem and depends on the subsystem, but gradually controls the subsystem. Because of the growth, the structure and functions of the subsystem are specialized, and as a result, some functions are supported and controlled by the upper system.

4) The Characteristics and Functions of the System

Three aspects distinguish the system in dealing with the complex of interacting elements: Number, species, and relations between elements. Of these, the cases of number and species can be expressed as cumulative or sum of individual elements that can be separated from each other, but the relationship between elements should be known as well as the elements. At this time, the former is referred to as summative and the latter as constitutive, representing the overall characteristics between them.

The meaning of the cumulative feature is that the elements have the same properties and can be represented by the sum of the features and behaviors of the elements. On the other hand, useful features rely on unique relationships within the complex. Therefore, to understand these characteristics, we need to know not only the parts but also the relationships between them. For example, the cumulative features are found in weight, a mass of molecules, heat (when considered to be the sum of molecular motion), and the constitutive features in chemical bonds.

In this respect, the whole, which is the core of the constitutional feature, is more than the sum of the parts, which means that the characteristics of the isolated part cannot explain the constitutional feature. Thus, the assumption of wholeness is essential because of its useful features. In other words, wholeness is established when their interaction combine the existing elements, not when they constitute a diffuse aggregate.

The assumption of wholeness is linked to the assumption of integration. The assumption of integration stipulates that the relations between the elements are very close and that the close relationship types are characteristic of all elements. Thus, the functional whole has the feature that the interrelationships between the components are very close and organic, so that changing some part inevitably changes the other part, sometimes the whole.

In conclusion, the characteristics of the system are the characteristics of the complex of the elements of the system; that is, the composite of elements has a cumulative character and a constitutive characteristic. However, when describing the characteristics of the system, what should be looked at in addition to its constitutive characteristics is that the whole is more than the sum of parts. This implies expressing aggregate characteristics that can not be found in a component.

Following the characteristics of the system, as shown above, the functions of the system are as follows. An important starting point in the general system theory is that the system is an open system that performs input and output functions. In other words, the system is distinguished from the closed system in that it is not isolated from the environment. All behaviors are within an open system, and all behaviors are assumed to be energy exchanges within or between systems. The specific functions and sizes performed by the system can be measured on a relative scale. If these exist in the system, they are called variables, and if they exist in the environment, they are called parameters.

Another important concept in general system theory is system maintenance and system regulation. The system tends to maintain a stable state among a large number of variables by performing significant functions. The system not only tries to stay in equilibrium but also tries to maintain a balance with the environment based on input and output. A system with this characteristic performs the following functions.

First, the system performs a function of adaptation. This function means that the system acquires human and material resources, information, and data from the environment processes it and distributes it.

Second, the system performs a function of goal attainment. This implies the ability to specify what the goal is to be pursued by the system and to specify the goal by organizing and utilizing all the resources procured from the environment to achieve it.

Third, the system performs a function of integration. It refers to the ability to coordinate and integrate the activities of the various subsystems and components that make up the system.

Fourth, the system performs a function of pattern maintenance. This function means that the system maintains a basic pattern and continuously creates and reproduces its values and norms.

3.1.3 The Relevance of General System Theory

1) The Critique of General System Theory

The Criticism of the general system theory is raised in two respects. One is the criticism of the basis on which the system theory is based, and the other is the criticism raised in terms of realistic or operational aspects. First of all, system theory or systematic app-roach is criticized from the starting point, despite the advantages of the theory. This can be seen in three ways:

First, it is a critique of the scientific method that forms the basis of the system theory as a criticism of the system theory, which is raised from the fundamental point of view. The problem raised from a fundamental point of view is still discussed in the philosophy of science or social science, which can be said to be the matter of comparing the similarities between social systems and physics/ biology. As a result, the system theory is dangerous because the dissimilarities of the social system are not ignored or clearly defined.

In other words, it is a criticism that the analytical method pursued by system theory lacks the accuracy to emphasize from the logical and linguistic viewpoint, the analysis method pursued by system theory lacks the accuracy emphasized from a logical and linguistic viewpoint, thus the result is doubtful. Therefore, it is a criticism that scientific research should be stopped until the system theory has a thorough formal system.

Notably, the scientific language system uses metaphor and analogy, and the problem is that metaphors and analogies are presented in various forms. To use metaphors and analogies, use them with sufficient risk factors removed. However, using metaphors in system theory that is partially formatted is a criticism that they have severe problems in methodology.

Second, the following criticism of the system theory is focused on the nature of the conceptual framework proposed by system theory. The systematic renovation that modern politics should pursue is all the more so in that it lies in exploring new ways and pioneering the realm of research to interpret old problems.

In order for the system theory to establish an analytical framework by introducing the concepts and theories of a system developed in biology and communication theory into the political analysis, it is necessary to have experimental expertise applied only to specific political subjects. Moreover, the analytical framework that has gone through this process emphasizes the need to integrate into the subject of politics through assumptions and theoretical orientation appropriate to the analysis of the political system.

Third, another critique of system theory is related to the reasons for adopting systematic analysis and also to fundamental criticism. For example, Eastern emphasizes that the political system should be understood as an analytical unit, not as an entity, in which the concept of a system is not set as a subject that is adapted to the real world. This is a matter related to the cognitive issue, which is the core problem of social science.

In addition to criticizing the rationale behind the theory, system theory has the following problems in terms of practical and operational aspects.

First, since subjectivity and prejudice determine the formation and application of the model, the validity of the model is not significant.

Second, the different levels of subsystems that make up the upper system are treated at the same level. Besides, the decision on the number of subsystems and the limitations on the process of input, conversion process, and output are too arbitrary. Thus, by treating the relationship between elements and elements in a macroscopic way, it can not explain the specific operating or behavioral aspects of the system, nor can it divide the whole phase into meaningful categories. In other words, system theory does not have the tools to analyze and dissect the contents of the system in detail.

Third, maintenance of the upper system is possible through a balance between subsystems, so it pursues balance maintenance. Therefore, it is impossible to introduce an imbalanced strategy for social reform. As a result, the system theory is weak in explaining the change or development with purposes, even though it is well explained about the state of survival and balance of the system. Of course, it is not that the system theory does not address changes.

However, the changes dealt with in the system theory are the changes that have emerged as a ripple effect through the parts, not a value-oriented change. In this sense, the system theory is not immune to conservatism and static.

Fourth, the system theory underestimates the independent role of the system. For example, when the administrative system holds the initiative and plays a leading role in development, it is not able to explain this phenomenon. In other words, the system theory values only the interdependent role between variables, so it neglects the independent role of variables. In other words, it overlooks the fact that some variables are highly dependent on others, while others are inherently independent.

Fifth, it is pointed out that if the system theory synthesizes the theories that are composed irrespective of the concept of the system, it becomes an unnatural theory and eventually loses the significance of the system theory.

In other words, when applying the system to political or administrative phenomena, it has side effects that can not deal with the problem that it wants to deal with. For example, the essential contents of political and administrative phenomena are power, rule, leadership, policymaking, efficiency, rationality, but the systematic approach is weak in dealing with such problems.

2) The Applicability of General System Theory

Despite its limitations, system theory has many advantages in terms of the applicability of the theory. From a political and sociological perspective, the system theory provides the convenience of integrating several partial analysis methods (coalition theory, exchange theory, role theory, value consensus) in the broad context of the existence of the system.

In particular, system theory suggests the source of concepts and models that can be of great help in empirical manipulation. There is also a practical advantage in that it can be applied to specific and essential areas to set hypotheses that can be empirically verified.

In conclusion, system theory can establish a general theory with universality because it presents general criteria for comparative analysis of various systems with diversity. Besides, the system theory is abstract because it deals with the object of study as a symbol, holistic in that the structure is not essential, dynamic in that it deals with changes, and practical in that it is interested in the performance of a task or function.

As a result, system theory can contribute to problem-solving and the rationalization of decision making, and it can contribute to the scientificization of the theory because it can predict and explain the administrative behavior more precisely through the use of extensive information theory.

3.2 New Public Administration Theory

3.2.1 The Background of New Public Administration Theory

1) The Reasons for the Emergence

The reason for the emergence of new public administration theory can be seen both in theoretical and practical aspects. From the theoretical point of view, it is possible to deduce the background of the emergence of the new public administration theory in terms of the repulsive aspect of the existing administrative theory with a low level of relevance or practical suitability as a theory.

Besides, in the practical sense, the problems inherent in the United States have exploded at once since the 1960s, and the new public administration theory has emerged as an alternative theory, with criticism that existing administrative theories cannot heal problems. More specifically, the two reasons for the emergence of the new public administration theory are as follows.

In the theoretical aspect, the background of the emergence of the new public administration theory is the reactionary atmosphere to the limitation of the theoretical relevance of the comparative and development administration theory and behavioralism which were the existing dominant administrative theory.

First, comparative administration theory and development administration theory, which contributed to the scientification of public administration, have played a significant role in enriching the academic reality of administration. In particular, the two theories contributed significantly to transforming public administration into a mature academic entity by applying a more relevant and sophisticated methodology to administrative phenomena, along with contributing to the scientificization of public administration.

However, despite their contribution, the comparative administration theory and development administration theory have begun to reveal its limitations due to inherent problems and contradictions.

Second, in the late 1960s, the frenzy of post-behavioralism began to put a brake on excessive behavioral approach and the necessity of quantitative and value-free oriented academic efforts for the scientificization of discipline.

For example, since administration itself is a value-loaded concept, criticism that the argument of behavioral theory that the value should be excluded from public administration research is criticized as a bowl without content. Finally, the current public administration, especially the behavioral theory centered on logical positivism, was centered on the inability to solve the pressing problems that arise in administrative reality for these reasons.

The next reason behind the emergence of the new public administration theory from the realistic point of view is the rebellious atmosphere due to the limitations of practical relevance of the comparative and development administration theory and behavioralism which was the dominant administrative theory.

In the 1960s, social problems that had been lurking in the United States since the Second World War began to erupt all at once. For example, there has been a turbulent field such as the failure to reach a national consensus following the intervention and expansion of the Vietnam War, urban riots, racial disputes, and deepening income inequality. To solve the problems, the Great Society program of the Johnson administration, which took effect in 1965, ended with a rosy fantasy.

The public's distrust and disappointment in the government and administration promptly amplified the need to create new values and demanded a new administrative paradigm to overcome them. This social atmosphere has also had a profound impact on the field of public administration. As a result, it is naturally necessary for the young scholars to consolidate a new academic system that can accommodate change and form a consensus on the limitation of the value-free with the quantitative approach.

2) The Development Process

The serious social problems that the United States has had a profound impact on the development of administrative theory. As mentioned, the value-free oriented academic attitude of behavioralism based on logical positivism has already lost its relevance for healing social problems. The comparative and development administration theory could no longer be a theory to cure the problems faced by the United States.

Comparative administrative and developmental administration were also a situation in which America could no longer heal its problems. These problems that American society has bred have driven political and administrative scientists to shift their attention from developing countries to developmental issues within American society. In 1967, scholars who were in a leading position in the field of public administration held a conference.

According to James Clyde Charlesworth, who was in charge of the chair, the purpose of this conference was to try a bold approach to public administration and to confirm the importance of public administration in a philosophical context. However, scholars and practitioners made sharp criticisms of the conclusions reached this meeting, and the dissatisfaction triggered the new public administration movement. In order to overcome this period and the crisis prevailing in academic and administrative fields, the American Society for Public Administration has tried various efforts.

As part of that, the first Minnowbrook Conference was held in 1968. In other words, a meeting was held in Minnowbrook, near Syracuse, New York, to establish the new paradigm that the times call for, to address the problem of the distributional justice in connection with the problem of the urban severe poor and the problem of racial divisions in the United States. As a result, a new paradigm of public administration, the new public administrative theory, was created in response to the times.

At the *Minnowbrook Conference on Administrative Problems* presided over by Dwight Waldo, the junior scholars harshly criticized the existing administrative theory for lacking the ability to prescribe social prescriptions for real issues. In particular, they raised the issue of the identity crisis of public administration, and as a new alternative, they focused on a normative theory that emphasizes social equity, humanitarian philosophy, relevant administrative research, and responsiveness to social change.

After this meeting, three important texts were published as a result. Several themes have been mentioned in this literature, some of which included content that was key to understanding the new public administration.

The representative literature published after the Minnowbrook Conference was *Toward a New Public Administration* edited by Frank Marini and *Public Administration in a Time of Turbulence* published by Dwight Waldo in 1971, and *Neighborhood Control in the 1970s* published by H. G. Frederickson in 1973. The oriented academic attitude of behavioralism based on logical positivism has already lost its relevance for healing social problems.

Among them, F. Marini pointed out that the critical themes of the Minnowbrook Conference were relevance, post-positivism, adaptation to the vortex environment, new forms of organization, and customer-oriented organization. As F. Marini pointed out, the value and ethics issues that emerged in the 1970s formed the academic base of the new public administration theory.

The new public administration theory has started with a new public administration movement led by young scholars, and practitioners who were dissatisfied with the traditional administrative theory and the realistic situation sought a new perspective. However, since the spirit, approach, and perspectives that emerged in the early days of the movement were more diversified than unified, it was a difficult task to explain it comprehensively and singly.

In the 1970s, the new public administration theory, which has established a theoretical system to some extent, was a new paradigm. It was challenging to say that it completely replaced the existing theory, but it was harmonized with the existing theoretical system with a strong influence on all fields of public administration.

3.2.2 The Content and Characteristics of New Public Administration Theory

1) The Concept of New Public Administration Theory

The new public administration movement was born in 1968 at the Minnowbrook Conference, which was sponsored by D. Waldo and was attended by young scholars and practitioners. It began to spread into a movement the following year by reaffirming it at a meeting of the American Society for Public Administration.

According to D. Waldo, scholars who attended the two conferences expressed common grievances about orthodox administration but stated that the claims were surprisingly different. Thus D. Waldo's statement implies that the nature of the new public administration was not uniform because it contained very diverse views.

Horace George Frederickson also referred to the diversity of views of the new public administration, similar to D. Waldo. However, H. G. Frederickson saw that the new public administration has a diversity of perspectives, but that there is no specific new public administration theory. Thus, the new public administration emphasized that it did not draw consensus on the new public administration theory, even though it completely ignored the traditional administrative theory and norms.

So, in the heterogeneity and diversity of the new public administration, what is the essence of novelty as a paradigm? To this end, let us take a look at how scholars classified as new public administration theorist look at the perspective of the new public administration discussed at the Minnowbrook Conference.

As mentioned, F. Marini, a representative of the new public administration scholars, discussed the relevance, post-positivism, adaptation to the vortex environment, new forms of organization, and customer-oriented organization. Richard S. Page assessed that, in particular, the following arguments were discussed, especially given that existing public administration did not provide prescriptive advice, i.e., sound normative value, to public administration scholars, practitioners, and citizens.

Public administration scholars and practitioners participating in the Minnowbrook Conference recognized the following. First, they should consider the value issue, and second, take responsibility for acting accordingly, and third, they should have a clear insight into the normative shortcomings implied by the public organization, administration or policy.

Finally, D. Waldo defined the nature of novelty as a normative theory, philosophy, social validity, and activism. Therefore, this means overcoming positivism and scientism in the passive side, and it can be understood that it is to find appropriate value from the standpoint of existentialism or phenomenology inactive aspect and realize it.

In summing up the scholars' view of the contents of the new public administration discussed at the Minnowbrook Conference, the new public administration scholars identified the proper normative value along with the pursuit of normative theory and emphasized change as a policy means to realize the value.

However, the normative theory in public administration is a theory about the value goal that public administration should pursue. In other words, it is a theory related to what public administration scholars and practitioners should do and what they should recommend to practitioners. Accordingly, new public administration scholars who want to pursue the normative theory needed to determine what value to pursue from the outset. However, the attitude of the new public administration scholars on the value issues was not clear from the beginning.

However, only H. G. Frederickson maintained a consistent attitude toward the value issues that the new public administration should pursue from the outset. For example, H. G. Frederickson emphasized the value of social equity, but he takes the position that he does not entirely ignore the traditional value of public administration-saving and efficiency.

Since the 1970s, the new public administration scholars have primarily taken a position of sympathy with H. G. Frederickson's claim. Carl J. Bellone, for example, emphasizes the traditional and new values of public administration at the same time, especially social equity as an essential new value. Therefore, the characteristics of the new public administration theory are, among other things, found in its emphasis on normative aspects: social equity.

The advocates of the new public administration movement started from the criticism that the current public administration is avoiding the issue of the times. Thus, the new public administration scholars argued that public administration should be a highly relevant discipline so that it can accurately recognize the situation of the times and present prescriptions for it.

In conclusion, the new public administration theory is a paradigm that emerged by young scholars who were dissatisfied with the current public administration seeking a new direction for the identity and the methodology of public administration. On the other hand, the emergence of the new public administration theory can be regarded as a neo-isolationism phenomenon, in which the attention of the public administration has returned to the problems in the United States from the problem of the underdeveloped country represented by the comparative administration theory and the development administration theory.

2) The Characteristics of New Public Administration Theory

As D. Waldo stated, the nature of the new public administration theory is not uniform but consists of a wide variety of views. In order to understand the meaning of the new public administration theory more detail, the characteristics of the new public administration theory will be described as follows.

■ New Public Administration Theory in the Normative Aspect

Allen Schick defined the characteristics of the new public administration theory as a new paradigm for pursuing appropriate social change while increasing the relevance in order to maximize social equity in the normative aspect.

Normative Character

The new public administration theory has rejected the traditional public administration, which has emphasized a value-neutral stance or procedural neutrality and has taken a position that emphasizes normative character in a new direction that administrative theory should pursue. In other words, the public administration must heal the illness of society. For this purpose, the new public administration is aiming at norm-oriented that values should be given first and foremost.

The reason why the new public administration theory emphasizes the normative nature of scholarship as follows. First, public administration or political science cannot maintain value neutrality. Second, public administration scholars should be an advocate for the underprivileged in society.

The Relevance

The relevance refers to the ability of an administrative theory to cope with or solve social problems. The administrative theory should be able to deal with various social problems facing society in order to improve relevance. The administrative organization should also be structured to have flexibility and adaptability suited to social change rather than the perfection of form in order to solve social problems.

In this respect, the emphasis on the Minnowbrook Conference was that the existing administrative theory is not suitable for relevance. Thus, the new public administration theory has developed the claim that the existing administrative theory lost its practical character and relevance so that it should develop the administrative capacity to cope with the rapidly changing modern society.

Social Equity

The new public administration theory particularly emphasized social equity. The reason for this is that, since the access capabilities of a specific group influenced the administrative services that have caused inequality in the past being, the administrative theory should establish an institutional mechanism to ensure equal benefits of administrative services. In other words, since the administration has should eliminate social inequalities, it is necessary to pursue social equity by providing better services for those at a social, political, and economic disadvantage.

Emphasis on Change

The new public administration theory emphasizes that change must be triggered in all parts to achieve social equity. Maintaining the society as it is now will result in creating an environment that is advantageous only to the ruling class. Therefore, it is necessary to change the system and the environment in order for the administration to escape the subjugation of the ruling class.

The new public administration theory contested the traditional organizational theory centering on the existing hierarchy and bureaucratic institutionalism in the way of change and argued for a reorganization into an anti-hierarchical and non-bureaucratic organizational model aimed at decentralization and expansion of participation.

■ Differences between the New Public Administration Theory and the Traditional Administration Theory

Another characteristic of the new public administration theory is the following when compared with the traditional administration theory.

Value Issues

Considering the value issues that public administration should pursue, the new public administration scholars sharply criticized the behavioralism and positivism of taking a value-neutral stance. Therefore, the new public administration scholars take post-behavioralism or phenomenological and existentialist position that they should actively confirm and create value and realize it, unlike the existing behavioralists.

The Relevance

Regarding the relevance of the public administration, the new public administration scholars criticize the fact that the existing administrative theory has ignored the fact that the least beneficiary class is treated as unequal discrimination in the political system. In other words, the existing administrative system and administrative theory have refused social justice for the minimum beneficiary class as a means of maintaining the status quo. Therefore, the new public administration scholars argued that the public administration should seek a relevant administration theory for the least beneficiary group in terms of social justice.

Social Equity

The new public administration theory should emphasize social equity, which is a value related to the social purpose of government by integrating the viewpoint of value and reality. In other words, public administration scholars and practitioners should strive for the benefit of the minimum beneficiary class, both inside and outside the administrative organization. To this end, it is necessary to develop and apply policy instruments, organizational structures, and management measures that can realize social equity. Moreover, they emphasize that the ideology and direction of social equity should be reflected in administrative theory and practice, as well as in administrative education and civil service education.

3) The Location of New Public Administration Theory

With the location problem of the new public administration theory or the establishment of relationships with the existing administrative theory, it is not entirely possible to deny existing administrative theories or norms, even if the characteristics of the new public administration theory are differentiated from those of the past administrative theories or norms. Besides, since the values pursued by the new public administration theory vary according to the scholars, it is also challenging to define the unified new public administration theory.

Therefore, since the contents contained in the new public administration theory are derived from the various values that have dominated the past administration, the new public administration theory should be understood in the context of the development of traditional public administration.

For example, the new public administration theory also includes the value of efficiency and saving, which was emphasized in the classic bureaucracy model. The problem is not in the value itself but in the difference between the way and the modality of achieving it. In other words, the value of efficiency and saving is not achieved only in such a way as the hierarchy, management control, authority, and centralization taking place in the traditional administrative model. Instead, loose control, loose bureaucracy, and de-authoritarian leadership can realize these values.

Besides, the rationality of decision-making, which is emphasized in the neo-bureaucratic model, is also implied in the new public administration theory. Other values such as worker satisfaction, personal growth, personal dignity, and civic choice, which are emphasized in the human relations model and the public choice model, are also related to the new public administration theory. Finally, these traditional administrative values are fused with the value of social equity, forming a model for the new public administration theory.

4) The Pursuit Value of New Public Administration Theory

Values such as efficiency, saving, and productivity, which were emphasized in traditional administration, are the dominant values that the administration should pursue under any conditions. In this respect, a series of values dominate the new public administration theory, which is above all, among other things, is rejecting value-neutral administrator and administrative theories. Also, in the new public administration theory, it is acknowledged that these administrative values are mutually competitive and have distinct reasons for their existence.

■ The Values Pursued by the New Public Administration Theory

The norms and values that characterize the new public administration theory include responsiveness, the participation of workers and citizens, social equity, civic choice, and administrative responsibility. They are urgently required values in American politics and administration and have normative and empirical support. However, the values that the new public administration theory intends to pursue can be summarized in terms of social equity. Social equity is not a concept to preach administrative ethics and morality but rather a concept to approach administrative theory and practice from a different point of view.

Equity in this respect is a crucial concept in understanding the current administration. Social equity, such as efficiency, saving, and productivity, should also be a criterion for evaluating public officials' behavior and decision-making and measuring the effectiveness of administration. This is because even though most of the critical policy decisions contain ethical content, ethical standards for public officials are not set.

There is no one's sole criterion of conduct in ethical matters, but decisions should be made in the direction of minimizing harmful side effects while gaining the maximum effect with the given resources. In addition, when politics and administration are open, people-oriented, and allow participation, the morality of administration will be guaranteed to the fullest extent, and the administration can realize social equity.

In the new public administration theory, the critical issue is whether social equity is being enhanced through public services. Generally, there is a tendency to assume the people as homogeneous and not admit the heterogeneity between individuals, which may be convenient, but logically and practically incorrect. In modern society, wealth and poverty, employment and unemployment, health and disease, knowledge and ignorance, hope and despair are found everywhere, and current administration presupposes a different situation.

In particular, While pluralistic governments are particularly favorable to bureaucracy and certain minorities, they are discriminatory against minorities who do not own political and economic resources. Inequality is found in any system, but if the administration can not solve the inequality, it is more likely to be abused as a means of suppressing deprived people, so the new public administration theory emphasizes equity.

Social equity will be a vital issue in future policy decisions. Public officials should develop standards and measures of equity and demonstrate their validity while understanding the impact of public services on the human dignity and well-being of citizens. Therefore, public servants' education should be structured to understand the concept of social equity, and public officials should carry out their duties while taking into account the social consequences of their work. To this end, the government must allow public officials to participate and to understand citizens' needs by interacting with election officials or the legislature daily.

In addition, civil servants should play the role of exploring and coordinating administrative countermeasures against social, economic and political changes, and their leadership, along with election officials or the legislatures, should systematically plan the process of change, and carry out their duties reasonably with the appropriate functions and service levels of the government in mind.

■ Structural Means for Value Realization

Structural means to embody the values pursued by the new public administration theory include decentralization, civic control, participation in decision making by workers, equal distribution of services, contracting, and delegation of authority. Moreover, management measures include interaction with employees and customers, education and training, acceptance of employee participation ethics, training for organizational development, adoption of the equity-based vocational ethics charter, the practice of minority protection, mitigation of monopolies in certain services, and measurement of performance by social class. For the realization of the values pursued by the new public administration in the contemporary context, the characteristics of the principal means presented as realistic alternatives are as follows.

First, participation in the process of setting goals and execution, which are meant by the new public administration theory, is not ending with a single vote act but is used as a broad concept. In other words, participation in the decision-making process of the administrative agency should be done even if it sacrifices administrative efficiency.

Second, the new public administration theory emphasizes on the distributional aspect by emphasizing administrative equality. Therefore, the new public administration theory is to consider as many variables as possible while dissatisfied with the limitations of quantitative approach such as the Planning Programming Budgeting Systems(PPBS), cost-benefit analysis, or system analysis. As a result, the assessment is much higher than the traditional assessment based on efficiency, and in this sense, the shift from cost-benefit analysis to cost-effectiveness analysis or policy output analysis is in the spotlight, which suggests what the new public administration theory pursues.

Third, the new public administration theory requires that conflicts with the outside world arising in the process of distribution within an organization be resolved by confrontation by the administrators who make some progress clear, rather than by gradual compromise or negotiation. Therefore, it advocates the attitude of value-oriented bureaucrats rather than value-neutral.

Fourth, the new public administration theory shows a clear difference from the traditional public administration in terms of how to look at the hierarchy existing in authority and organization. The new public administration theory also does not presume a society without a complete hierarchy. However, it is a position to revise the traditional hierarchy both in theory and in practice. In this respect, it emphasizes organizational forms, such as project organization and matrix organization.

Fifth, the new public administration theory was influenced by the open system theory. Thus, on the assumption that openness should be maximized between the organization and the environment, organizational development, such as sensitivity training for organizational participants, is presented as a reform plan.

In conclusion, the new public administration theory does not deny the importance of values such as efficiency and saving that have been emphasized in traditional public administration. The new public administration theory can be found in its emphasis on poverty, inequality, and injustice, even if the government is efficient and economical. Thus, the new public administration theory is meaningful in that it emphasizes the importance of social equity more than any theory in the ethical dimension of public services.

3.2.3 The Relevance of New Public Administration Theory

1) The Limitations of New Public Administration Theory

Emerging in the context of re-examination of a vast bloated bureaucracy, a reduction-oriented prescription for it, and era dilemma that cannot be solved without intervening in the problems of administrative value and ethics, the new public administration theory seems to have an epochal validity in terms of its background of birth. Notably, all the social problems such as poverty problems and distorted allocation of wealth, resources and opportunities, distorted social equity, and human rights violations that are difficult to solve, even if these problems require new prescriptions and perspectives.

The new public administration theory emerged in this period, criticizing the existing behavioralism and expressing value-oriented. They were in the position that they made value a top priority in the study of public administration and that they could not think of it as public administration that left the value issue. Like Dwight Waldo's assessment, the new public administration theory was a tentative prescription that appeared as a product of the times and has had a massive impact on existing public administration.

However, there has been little accumulation of the new public administration theory's alleged value-oriented as a theory, and the results of the study have not produced much success either. Although the spirit is confident, it can be said that it cannot escape from the lack and emptiness of its contents. That is, it flows in a direction that lacks methodology and is rhetorical.

The new public administration movement made efforts to outline a philosophical alternative that could replace logical positivism by various scholars for several years after the first Minnowbrook Conference to overcome these problems. For example, Robert B. Denhardt and Michael M. Harmon et al. have presented an interpretative, analytical, and critical approach for research and exploration as an alternative.

These alternatives, however, were not discussed extensively at the second Minnowbrook Conference later held in 1988. Nothing appeared at the second Minnowbrook Conference that would lead to the development of post-positivism, other than Hamon's criticism of decision-making as a criterion for the study of organizational theory.

Aside from M. M. Harmon's critique of decisionism as a standard for research on organizational theory, nothing at all has emerged at the Second Minnowbrook Conference to elaborate the theory of post-positivism. In other words, the new public administration theory has been shattered by innocent beliefs that were optimistic about many of the events that took place during the 1970s and 1980s, revealing their insignificant ability to solve.

Especially, since the new public administration theory is based on the recognition of the situation in the 1960s and 1970s, it is inevitable to think whether all the contents of the new public administration scholars still have meaning at the time when the rapidly changing situation like that time does not continue. In addition, the new administration theory is not a 'new' administration theory in a complete sense, but it is also criticized that it is an effort to approach the administrative phenomenon from a different perspective from the past.

Finally, the ideal state of the normative views that the new public administration scholars claim cannot be denied. For example, values such as responsiveness and civic participation are desirable, but the limitations of the new public administration theory can be seen in that there are many difficulties in realizing these values.

2) The Applicability of New Public Administration Theory

The new public administration theory challenged the paradigm of traditional public administration by emphasizing the normative rather than value-neutral, the prescription rather than the technical, and the customer-oriented administration and public administration rather than the institution-oriented.

At the same time, the normative orientation of the new public administration theory is related to the critical administration or action theory that emerged around the 1980s. In particular, the value of social equity, emphasized by the new public administration theory has led to a change in the direction of value orientations that the administration should pursue, which has been neglected by the traditional public administration.

In other words, the theoretical applicability of the new public administration theory is very significant in that among the values that administration should pursue, and it emphasizes that equality, equity, and relevance are as important administrative values as efficiency, effectiveness, and rationality. Besides, the validity of the new public administration theory is beyond dispute in that it emphasizes the realization of social equality and equality in order to realize the ultimate value of human life.

However, the new public administration theory should be placed as a new paradigm of administrative philosophy, humbly accepting its abilities and limitations, and re-establishing values required by the administration of the new era. Also, it should be able to help broaden the academic horizon of public administration by contributing to the upgrading of the public administration faced with the identity crisis to a more responsive academic system.

Chapter V

Public Administration in the Reversal Period

1. The Story of the Public Administration in the Reversal Period

The 1970s, when the United States met, was an era of a vortex. The deepening of the civil rights movement, the Vietnam War, the Watergate scandal, and the energy crisis began to emerge as distrust of the government's ability and performance and demanded a new paradigm different from the old one. In other words, if the 1960s were a time when the administration promised to expand and grow, then the 1970s was a time when everything was reversed and reviewed.

For example, the Nixon administration established the Environmental Protection Agency in 1970 as an organization dedicated to environmental issues, while the Nixon administration abolished the Planning Programming Budgeting Systems(PPBS) from the federal government in the same year.

The Great Society program, first presented in the 1965 presidential race and ambitiously promoted by the Johnson administration, failed. Moreover, before the aftershocks disappeared, President Richard Milhous Nixon's resignation from Watergate scandal and his failure in Vietnam drove the United States into a chaos field.

Besides, the financial crisis facing the state and local governments created a new atmosphere called cutback management. Therefore, instead of the concept of market failure, the concept of government failure or a non-market failure has emerged, and the cutback management theory based on the ideology of a small government began to spread due to the influence of neo-conservativism or neoliberalism-based on resource shortages and financial crisis.

Recognizing that the administration is in a period of revolution, Dwight Waldo held the Minnowbrook Conference in 1968, which later led to the birth of new administration. In 1971, Frank Marini, then editor of the *Public Administration Review*, edited the papers and published them under the title *New Public Administration: Minnowbrook Perspective*. The main issue addressed at the Minnowbrook Conference was the question of the relevance of administration and how public administration should change in the face of the challenges of the 1970s.

Vincent A. Ostrom also pointed out the intellectual crisis of American public administration and suggested that public choice theory should be introduced into the public administration as an alternative to overcome this problem. He proposed to shift the focus of the public administration from traditional bureaucracy and the Wilsonian administrative model to the service delivery system.

Meanwhile, the evaluation work has begun to go brisk amid growing criticism of the Great Society Program pursued by the Johnson administration. However, the views surrounding the evaluation work of the government work were divided into positive and negative perspectives. Typically, scholars such as Aron B. Wildavsky showed a contrary view from the standpoint that evaluation work was not accessible due to the unique nature of government work, whereas most scholars were active in evaluating government programs.

Aron Bernard Waldavsky, for example, pointed to the difficulty of evaluating public programs in a dynamic political environment in a 1972 paper titled "The Self Evaluating Organization" published in *American Public Administration Review*. According to him, evaluation involves change, which is what the organization hates most. From the manager's point of view, it is harmful for the evaluation, and the internal strategy accordingly is focused on avoiding it as much as possible. So, the evaluation work was not easy to achieve the intended effect.

However, despite A. B. Wildavsky's argument, the assessment of government work has begun to form a trend. In 1967, the publication of the *Evaluative Research*, which summarized the theory of evaluation by Columbia University's Edward Suchman, was a signal to announce this. In the book, he argued that evaluation is a field of study and that scholars should study evaluation research and evaluation practices in a general context beyond the scope of application of evaluation in various specialized fields.

Since the publication of E. Suchman, the evaluation research have begun to be active in various aspects in the 1970s. Later, Carol H. Weiss published *Evaluation Research: Methods for Assessing Program Effectiveness* in 1972, which is rated as the best introduction to the sub-fields of the evaluation research.

The General Accounting Office(GAO), which was under the influence of Elmer B. Staats, was also an extended scope of accounting, contributing significantly to improving the quality and value of program evaluation by forming evaluation criteria through vigorous program evaluation.

Many states began to establish legislative appraisal committees in similar organizations in line with the philosophy pursued by the General Accounting Office and in 1976 the Colorado State Government became the first state to enact the sunset law. The position of evaluation that has been developed has emerged as an essential part of administration by the mid-1970s. Policy analysis is also an area that emerged as a response to the failed problems that occurred in the 1960s.

Typically, Jeffrey L. Pressman and Aron B. Wildavsky published a case study of the federal program conducted in the city of Auckland under the title *Implementation*. The gist of their argument is that policy planning and policy analysis were not considering the difficulties of implementation. So their main focus was on how a close link between policy and implementation could be formed. The title of the book published by them was of the entire contents that it seems to compress.

For reference, the original title of this book was as follows. *Implementation: How Great Expectations in Washington Are Dashed in Oakland; Or, Why It is Amazing that Federal Programs Work at All: This Being a Saga of the Economic Development Administration As Told by Two Sympathetic Observers Who Seeks to Build Morals on a Foundation of Ruined Hopes.*

In 1972, when policy analysis emerged as a new area of public administration, a national shock event commonly referred to as the Watergate scandal occurred. The aftermath of the Watergate scandal was once again a reflection of what is required of the administrative presidency.

That is, since the 1930s, administrative development has been tailored to the administration's concentration and control of power. Although problems have been resolved to some extent, it was an opportunity to reflect on this with lessons on what could happen if the politician abused centralized power, as seen in the Watergate case.

As part of this response, Frederick C. Mosher, who was then president of the American Society for Public Administration, submitted a report entitled "Watergate: Implications for Responsible Government" aimed at sanctioning the Nixon administration's abuse of executive and administrative power at the request of the Senate.

However, what is important about this report is that the concept of ethics and public office has brought about an opportunity to strengthen after this incident. In other words, there was a need for educational institutions to pay more attention to ethical issues in the public sector. As a result, *the Ethics in Government Act* was enacted in 1978.

The 1970s can also be said to be an era of the financial crisis with scarcity, and the changes in budget reform were more characteristic than other periods. The next step in the budget reform from this point of view was the realization of a Zero-based budgeting system. This system, introduced by James E. Carter, Jr. when he was governor of Georgia, was an election pledge to introduce a Zero–based budgeting system when he became a presidential candidate in 1976. Also, when he took office in 1977, he ordered the federal government to apply it.

In particular, Peter A. Phyrr, who introduced it when J. E. Carter was a governor, published the "Zero-Base Approach to Government Budgeting" in the *American Public Administration Review* in 1977, introducing the theory and methodology of the Zero-based budgeting system. However, the Carter administration adopted the Zero-based budgeting system as a reaction to the Planning Programming Budgeting Systems(PPBS), which was overwhelming in the 1960s, is entering the path of failure at a faster pace than the Planning Programming Budgeting Systems.

The reason for this is that the Zero-based budgeting system was to be very radical and most hastily distributed than the reform of the previous budget system. Moreover, in times of severe resource shortages, the Zero-based budgeting system had little advantage in terms of utility, which was also one of the reasons for the failure.

As a result, Aron B. Wildavky and Allen Schick claimed that the budget system had failed. The Zero-based budgeting system was officially abolished from the central government as the Carter administration stepped down. However, at the level of the state or local government, the techniques of this budget system were partially used. If the 1960s were a time of optimistic experiment on the administration, the 1970s was a time when everything was integrated and skeptical.

2. The Representative Scholars in the Reversal Period

The characteristics of the development process of administrative theory in this period are as follows in the positions of representative scholars.

2.1 Frederick C. Mosher's Professionalism

Frederick C. Mosher published "Democracy and the Public Service" in 1968 and "The Public Service in the Temporary Society" in *American Public Administration Review* in 1971. F. C. Mosher's consistent stance is that as long as the merit system continues, professionalism will expand, and the professionalism of American public administration has risen remarkably. For example, American public administration is at a considerable level of quantitatively or qualitatively, which is evidenced by the level of demand or policy in the United States.

In his book published in 1968, he looked at how these factors have changed the nature and content of merit system, referring to changes in the professionalism, public service organizations, career civil service systems, and democratic values based on equal employment that form the basis of American personnel administration. As a result, he has found that there was a close relationship between them, but he did not think that a pure form of career system was the most desirable system.

Conversely, he has raised serious questions about whether the career system would be desirable to be used as a means to realize other social values, in addition to the value of efficiency. Therefore, he emphasized that the field of personnel administration in this aspect has not only a technical aspect but also a philosophical one.

Meanwhile, in a paper published in 1971, F. C. Mosher thought that professionalism was the most differentiated field in the new category of public services. In other words, professionalism has been developed by the needs of the different occupations to overcome social, technical, and managerial problems and has continued to develop professionalism through functional interdependence.

If this trend continues in the future, experts in the American government, whether direct or indirect, will account for about two-fifths of the total members. Therefore, he predicted that the relationship between the expansion of public policy and the resulting professionalism of personnel management would continue to increase functional interdependence. However, professionalism, in terms of professional skills, is under increasingly heavy pressure even in its categories.

2.2 Horace George Frederickson's Social Equity

Horace George Frederickson was one of the three members who were in charge of the preparation for the meeting when Dwight Waldo held the Minnowbrook Conference in 1968. However, he did not publish a separate paper at the conference. Then, when Frank Marini published the *New Public Administration: Minnowbrook Perspective* in 1971, he published a paper titled "Toward a New Public Administration" that contained his views on the new public administration movement in this book. From then on, H. G. Frederickson has played a role as a new public administration scholar and a pioneer of the new public administration movement.

H. G. Frederickson emphasized social equity and the delivery of public services as a new role for administration in this paper. In order to do this, he argued that the future administration should increase high responsiveness, customer-oriented, prescription, and universality in the direction it should aim for. Thus, he named the second-generation behavioralism, the administrative movement and the administrative scholars who are aiming for a new direction, as the new public administration movement.

H. G. Frederickson also argued that the new public administration movement demanded an administrator who could vigorously pursue social equity, instead of the traditional impersonal or neutral bureaucrat emphasized in bureaucracy. He was interested in new organizational theories and organizational behavior similar to other new public administration scholars in the case of organizational views, among which he showed great interest in decentralized structures that Warren G. Bennis and others have emphasized since the 1960s.

The administrative values that H. G. Frederickson argues have had a profound impact on the critical public administration and action theory in the 1980s. Especially the concept of social equity had a powerful influence on shaping new administrative ideology.

2.3 Carol H. Weiss's Evaluation Study

Carol H. Weiss opened a new horizon in the area of assessment in 1972 by publishing the *Evaluation Study: Methods for Assessing Program Effectiveness*. She raised several critical issues in the book, ranging from questions about the purpose and use of evaluation research and the choice and exchange of neutrality between inside and outside the assessment. C. H. Weiss can be particularly meaningful in raising methodological, political, and administrative issues that are controversial in program evaluation. In other words, she tried to find out whether the policy process genuinely reflected the policy evaluation research as scientific research.

The contents intended by C. H. Weiss are divided mainly into two main parts: the provision of the purpose of the assessment, along with the question of limitations or problems of the assessment as well as the other. Her view on the purpose of an evaluation is presented in the second chapter, The Purpose of Evaluation. For example, the purpose of evaluation research is first to evaluate existing policies or programs empirically, secondly to provide feed-back information to policymakers, and third, to secure accountability based on the evaluation.

Next, the problem she raised is the problem or limitation of evaluation, pointing out that past policy evaluation studies have not played a role and function as scientific research. Based on this, policy evaluations and program evaluations were not achieved in a value-neutral or value-exclusive situation because policy evaluation activities are carried out in the political arena.

In other words, she pointed out that the biggest obstacle to policy assessment activity is the fact that that activity cannot rule out the political impact, as policy assessment activities are carried out in the political arena. Therefore, she was concerned that the results of policy assessments carried out by policy evaluators are likely to be utilized under these political influences or requirements.

Of course, she did not claim that all of the existing evaluation studies were political. However, she pointed out the realistic limitations. That is, the pessimistic argument that the existing assessment research is not deviating from politics should under-estimate the objectivity or scientification of the assessment research. Therefore, she suggested that internal evaluation is more desirable than external evaluation as an alternative to enhance the effectiveness of evaluation research.

C. H. Weiss began with the premise that policy evaluation and program assessment cannot escape politically by inherently having political implications. Thus, she emphasized that in order to improve utility and fairness in evaluation research, it is necessary to have a more thorough understanding of how policies and programs were formed and implemented, and the structure and process of the institutions, and furthermore, social conditions.

C. H. Weiss's view of policy evaluation may not be a new argument. For example, the problem of political implication in policy evaluation was about a real problem for policy evaluators. It is important to note, therefore, that as she argues, the intensity of politics may vary depending on the type of policy or program, rather than all of the evaluation studies having political consideration.

At the same time, she can hardly escape criticism in that she neglected the problem of contributing to academic development through the development and application of the evaluation methodology based on the assessment study, one of the fundamental purposes of evaluation research, by highlighting the political nature of evaluation research too much. It is particularly problematic that she reduced the scope of the evaluation study in that she excluded the contribution of external evaluation by overemphasizing internal evaluation due to the political nature of the evaluation study.

2.4 Vincent A. Ostrom's Public Choice

Vincent A. Ostrom, in conjunction with James McGill Buchanan and Gordon Tullock in 1963, held an academic conference on the subject *The No-Named Field of Public Administration* from a political economy point of view and introduced it to the *American*

Public Administration Review.

V. A. Ostrom has since been striving to incorporate these new fields with existing public administration. The result was a paper titled "Public Choice: A Different Approach to the Study of Public Administration," published in the *American Public Administration Review* with his wife, Elinor Ostrom. Two years later, the book was published in the context of the public choice theory, expanding this thesis. It was *The Intellectual Crisis in American Public Administration.*

V. A. Ostrom was a scholar who was consistently skeptical about the relevance of the paradigm of existing public administration and devoted himself to the exploration of public choice theory as a new paradigm. In this book, V. A. Ostrom diagnosed that the current public administration is in the crisis of paradigm because of the following reasons or signs.

First, there has been too much disagreement over the dominant theory. Second, public administration scholars are more willing to participate in methodological experiments. Third, public administration scholars are expressing dissatisfaction with the existing paradigm. Fourth. Fundamentally, there is a controversy about epistemological issues. Therefore, V. A. Ostrom sought the democratic administration paradigm as an alternative with the necessity of public choice as a new paradigm for these reasons.

The intellectual crisis of public administration, which V. A. Ostrom means, started from the recognition of the limitations of the paradigm inherent in traditional public administration theory. The main reason why the existing public administration theories fail to solve urban problems, environmental problems, racial issues, and fiscal crises of the United States, which began to worsen since the 1960s, is that their paradigms are amid limitations.

As a result, V. A. Ostrom presented a paradigm of democratic administration based on public choice theory, along with criticism of the paradigms of classical public administration theory. For example, V. A. Ostrom has argued for a multi-dimensional organizational arrangement that has the characteristics of overlapping jurisdiction and dispersal of authority as an alternative to the bureaucratic organization, which can reflect the preferences of the society members as much as possible, considering the diversity and external effects of public goods.

3. The Representative Theory in the Reversal Period

The representative administrative theory that emerged in the reversal period of public administration is public choice theory. The background and characteristics and contents of the theory that led to the formation of the public choice theory are as follows.

3.1 Public Choice Theory

3.1.1 The Background of Public Choice Theory

The term public choice theory began to appear in modern social science in the 1960s. In November 1963, J. M. Buchanan and G. Tullock held a conference on *Political Economy*, advocating the need to apply the economic discussion to the collective, political and social policy-making behavior and public choice theory began to emerge as a new paradigm in social science.

Public choice theory is an attempt to study the interactions of political institutions through underlying assumptions and approaches to human beings in economics. In other words, the public choice theory is an attempt to approach the decision-making behavior that takes place outside the scope of the market economically. Thus, it is the theory that emerged to economically analyze and grasp the aim of decision-making behavior that takes place in political and administrative domains under the premise that humans are thoroughly rational in pursuing self-interest.

In this context, the public choice theory has focused its primary attention on the failure factors of the government in the political and administrative sciences to verify whether governments or political organizations have met political standards of efficiency or equity, or to verify why they have failed.

Meanwhile, when the public choice theory emerges as a new paradigm in social sciences, a group of political scientists has raised a substantial question about what existing political science is doing and why there is no analytical tool in the tradition of political science. So they have begun to pursue the task of finding its root in traditional political philosophy.

As a result, they have revealed that similar attributes and axioms have been inherent in the tradition of politics, in which the public choice theory has already emphasized. Therefore, this fact emphasizes that the public choice theory is not a monopolistic paradigm which is formed only in economics in the methodology, but that it has earlier been formed and developed in the development course of traditional political philosophy.

However, since the traditional political philosophy has been mainly concerned with issues such as the formation of government or nation following the conditions of the times, it was inevitably cut off after such conditions were achieved to some extent. In the end, the public choice theory is a new paradigm emerging to solve today's problems, which reveals the government failure, which is the result of the times' situation in another meaning.

3.1.2 The Background of Contents and Characteristics of Public Choice Theory

1) The Concept of Public Choice Theory

It is not easy to define the concept of public choice theory, that is, what the public choice theory is. The main reason for the difficulty in defining the concept of public choice theory is that the genealogy or roots of the public choice theory are complex. For example, the roots of the public choice theory originate from the 17th-century political thinker Thomas Hobbes, and economics is rooted in the work of French mathematician Jean-Charles Borda.

In addition, a group of political scientists and economists who attended a conference on the political economy led by J. M. Buchanan and G. Tullock in November 1963. However, they failed to name for the topic of the end-of-the-line meeting and named and closed it as *No-name conference* also showed that it is difficult to conceptualize the public choice theory.

However, although it is difficult to conceptualize the public choice theory, it seems that there is a consensus among scholars that the nature of public choice theory exists halfway between political science and economic science. From this point of view, the contents defined by scholars for the conceptualization of public choice theory are as follows.

Dennis C. Mueller defined public choice theory as an economic study of nonmarket decision-making or as an area of application of economics to political science. J. M. Buchanan characterizes public choice theory as an empirical attempt to enhance understanding of complex institutional interactions in the political domain by applying sophisticated approaches and tools developed in economic theory to political, governmental, or public economic sectors.

V. A. Ostrom & E. Ostrom defined public choice theory as a theory of various decision-making arrangements affecting public goods, which are the products of public institutions. In conclusion, the concept of public choice theory defined by various scholars is considered as a series of attempts to study the interaction of political and administrative institutions by applying economic approaches or tools to political and administrative science.

2) The Content and Characteristics of Public Choice Theory

The main characteristics of the public choice theory are as follows.

First, the public choice theory has a character of political economy. Therefore, it values the public goods and services produced by policies and emphasizes their publicness, taking a critical stance on applying economic logic in the private economic sector as it is.

Second, the public choice theory seeks the cause of government failure in that the government bureaucracy exerts an exclusive influence on the production and supply of public goods. The traditional government bureaucracy that exclusively supplies public services is viewed as an institutional device that can not respond sensitively to the demands of citizens due to the influence of organized pressure groups and at the same time suppresses the choice of citizens as consumers.

Accordingly, the public choice theory argues that the government should provide public services that respect the preferences and choices of individual citizens and that it is only possible to increase the administrative responsiveness by providing public services through competition. In the end, the public choice theory regards the government as a producer of public goods, and citizens as consumers of public goods, and from this viewpoint, the supply and production of services that can minimize costs and maximize the benefits of citizens are possible through the market economy of the public sector.

Third, the public choice theory emphasizes that the government have an ability in utilizing various organizational arrangements suitable for providing various public goods and public services. In other words, it emphasizes that the supply of public goods and services depends on the decisions of various decision-makers, and values the long-term political feasibility. V. A. Ostrom emphasizes the usefulness of multi-organizational devices in the case of government organizations that provide public goods, and these institutional devices imply a mechanism to resolve conflicts among agencies and agreements considering diversity among agencies.

However, the most crucial concept in the institutional apparatus is that the overlapping system can better respond to the interests of the relevant groups due to the problem of the dispersion of authority and the overlapping of jurisdiction. Accordingly, the main factors that make up the public choice theory are the principle of behavior such as voters, politicians, bureaucrats, and interest groups participating in the political decision-making process, and the distribution of resources and income.

In this regard, the public choice theory is a new attempt to overcome the problems presented by the existing administrative order and administrative theory and is concerned with the establishment of institutional devices that can sensitively respond to the diverse needs and preferences of citizens.

Fourth, the public choice theory emphasizes the spill-over effects of policy. The positive effect of policy means that the effects initially intended and expected by a policy-maker are realistically realized. Besides, negative effects mean that unintended side effects occur.

3) The Genealogy of Public Choice Theory

It is not easy to classify the development history or development process of public choice theory. It adds to the difficulty in considering the development history since the etymology of public choice theory initially was been by economists, and that similar historical backgrounds existed in the traditional political philosophy that had been overlooked as an incidental consequence of its development. So in this chapter, both the development process created in terms of economics and the development process developed in terms of political philosophy are described at the same.

■ Economic Genealogy

The criterion for examining the economic origin of public choice theory has been from the economic depression of the 1930s when market failures were being discussed in earnest. The main reason for the discussion to begin from this point is that as the conventional Smithonian liberal fiscal theory reveals the limitations, the Keynesian school and other forms of fiscal theory centered around the European continent emerged as an alternative to this.

However, what is vital in exploring the roots of public choice theory is not the emergence of the Keynesian, but the kind of study of continental-centered public goods that have developed public economics today. These were the areas of concern that they raised.

First, it was about the optimal budget theory, such as how much resources the government should allocate for the production of public goods.

Second, it was the problem was the decision-making of the financial authority, which is the most efficient way to share the costs required for the production of public goods. The two approaches to solve these problems are the welfare economic approach and the collective choice approach discussed in the political economy. However, the two approaches have evolved to be a mixture, though they are distinct from each other. As a result, while welfare economics has bridged the gap between economic markets and Pareto optimality, the collective choice theory has evolved to emphasize political interactions based on non-market decision theory that welfare economics have neglected.

The welfare economics study for the optimal allocation of public goods is divided into three categories.

First, it is a marginal utility approach developed by using the theory of taxability centered on Arthur Cecil Pigou. Second, it is a voluntary exchange approach developed by using the theory of tax profits as the center of Knut Wicksell and others. Third, the pure public goods model developed by Paul A. Samuelson and Richard Musgrave as an individualistic approach.

Among the welfare economics approaches, it is the voluntary exchange approach model that has influenced modern public choice theory. For example, while Erik Lindahl focused on public goods theory, K. Wicksell focused primarily on collective choice and public finances. In particular, K. Wicksell regarded the government as a compensation process for the exchange between citizens and viewed the political decision on resource allocation in a democratic society as being determined by a vote by an individual.

As a result, the ideal political decision-making method is a situation where the outcome of the vote is absolute unanimity, but it is impossible to be realistic. So K. Wicksell proposed relative unanimity, which requires two-thirds or more or more rigid 5/6 in a second-best manner. This decision-making method has had a profound impact on J. M. Buchanan and G. Tullock since then. It has also influenced positive public choice theory, such as how to decide by voting, among public choice theories.

Next, the collective choice theory also has its roots in economics, but the game theory that has been developed since John von Neumann and Oskar Morgenstern and the utility theory based on macroeconomics has driven the promotion of its development.

According to Duncan Black, which incorporates the collective choice theory into the context of political interactions, its roots have reached the present, beginning with J.-C. Borda. This position then affected Kenneth H. Arrow and Anthony Downs. In particular, A. Downs reconstructed the methodological individualism, an ancient method of analysis, and established a deductive model of how democratic politics worked and applied the maximized principle of utility to politics and administration. Later, in terms of rationality and self-interest, it was succeeded to Mancur Olson, who explained the theory of collective action.

K. Arrow expressed the common attributes of collective choice theorists as follows: They have been paying attention to the problem of aggregating personal preferences in a given environment, namely, how to aggregate choices of personal preferences into a collective choice.

■ Political Philosophical Genealogy

In the history of political philosophy, the position of epistemology has been divided into mechanismus(mechanism), chemismus (chemism), teleologie(teleology) according to the relation between universality and relativity of cognition, and the cognitive ability of human mind as the organizer of recognition. Therefore, scholars see the history of epistemological confrontation in political philosophy as the process of the mutual confrontation and unification of these three epistemologies.

Among these, mechanismus emerged against the theological and abstract universalism which advocates the divine right of kings. It is the epistemology that shares the most with the methodological elements of the public choice theory discussed today.

Mechanismus takes the relativistic epistemology that human beings are identified with nature and that all perceptions are established only through sensory experience. So it stands for naturalism and objectivism, that the same physical and natural laws govern perception subjectivity and perception objectivity. Thus, everything is nothing more than a quantitative difference, and all phenomena, like natural phenomena, are perceived as the immutable fact that simple repetition continues.

In the history of political philosophy, this pioneer of such epistemology was Thomas Hobbes. He created a mathematical-mechanical view and laid the foundations for methodological individualism under the concept of instrumental rationality. T. Hobbes' epistemology has since been extended to Baruch de Spinoza, David Hume, and Alexander von Humboldt, which can be called Hobbist. The methodological root of the public choice theory that has been embedded in their perceptions, here is the following.

T. Hobbes developed the theory from the analysis of human nature based on the concept of instrumental rationality. The right behavior for humans is an act of making him conform to self-interest, and self-interest oriented instinct is a common attribute of all humans. Therefore, human instinct makes human being the creator of endless activity and can pursue a specific purpose, and all the actions that human beings want and pursue are regarded as useful.

On the other hand, he viewed the act of causing hatred or fear in humans as evil, and good and evil have various meanings according to individual purposes. For example, all humans pursue their good so that they may do evil to others, regardless of their own will. By this, humans became interested in the natural right because of the need to protect themselves from the evil done by others, and the passion or desire to pursue good.

The law of nature derived from T. Hobbes' epistemological basis is immutable and has an eternal character. Humans have come to contract with the state in the belief that it is in their best interest to keep it. Therefore, T. Hobbes' law of nature emphasizes the fact that it was created by humans, not by God's command discussed in the medieval god-centric and cosmic perspective.

In the end, T. Hobbes is in line with the methodology of the public choice theory discussed today by taking the standpoint of methodological individualism that the basic unit of analysis of the state in terms of cognition must be an individual.

B. Spinoza's epistemological attributes were Hobbist and Cartesianism. Not only did B. Spinoza developed a systematic philosophy under the influence of Réne Descarte, but he owed much to his formula in human nature and governmental studies, even though there was a difference in degree with T. Hobbes.

B. Spinoza took a similar stance to T. Hobbes in his underlying assumption for humans. He also considered human motivation to be caused by interest or desires, which were an essential phenomenon for humans. He also emphasized empirical obligations to political scientists in a prescriptive sense, such as how to operate the structure of the political organization or how to cope with the change.

In particular, he classified the types of decision making as constitutional and operational or ordinary law in matters of collective decision making at the government level. Moreover, he suggested that the simple majority rule should be applied at the operational level and that the total agreement should be obtained or at least relative unanimity should be applied at the constitutional level in the decision-making method. This method has had a profound effect on the voting approach, which is the approach type of public choice theory.

D. Hume further developed the perception of self-interest centered human nature that T. Hobbes and B. Spinoza assumed. D. Hume's fundamental perception, called the natural history approach, attempted to explain the law of history by defining selfish activity itself as good or virtuous, as a principle of human nature, and clarifying a selfish source. D. Hume regarded the products of hedonic activity consumed by humans as passions.

Humans have the instinct to obtain such passion, which is that history is the accumulation of these passions. Therefore, D. Hume, taking a pluralistic stance on human happiness, regarded only the effort for the self-fulfillment of individuals as the principal value that can justify a free society. D. Hume's individualistic and self-interest oriented values are considered to be a driving force of economic activity, having a profound impact on the areas of epistemology and politics as well as on economic philosophy

In addition to D. Hume, A. v. Humboldt, as an enlightenment thinker, also provides a glimpse into the roots of public choice theory. His approach, which adopts the individualistic and economical approach in the way of describing the state, can be seen in his idea of the state. The state is a necessary evil, and the function of the state is to take only a simple role of protection against the lives and property of citizens.

The state should only be involved in eliminating or reducing the external costs of private conduct to explain this in an economical approach. A. v. Humboldt's approach to the state, therefore, is that the state should not engage in activities beyond its scope, even if there are externalities due to private acts. A. v. Humboldt's ideas are linked to laissez-faire political philosophy, which is in the sense that it tries to approach the economy in order to emphasize individual freedom for the state.

Finally, Léon Duguit, who emerged as a reaction to the concept of general will by Jean-Jacques Rousseau, also reveals many of the features discussed above, which demonstrate that there has been epistemology that public choice is oriented toward within the realm of political philosophy.

4) The Basic Axiom of Public Choice Theory

It is not easy to identify the fundamental axiom or methodological integrity pursued in public choice theory. This is because the field of public choice theory is still at a stage where it is gradually spreading the focus of its interests and research.

However, despite the circumstances of public choice theory, commonalities are inherent in the methodology, which is the axiom of methodological individualism. The following is a brief description of what the axiom of methodological individualism means and which functions it performs in the substantive domain.

■ Methodological Individualism

According to Friedrich August von Hayek, individualism is a

significant theory of society that rejects social analysis in principle and is an attempt to understand the source of determining human social life. Thus, individualism does not mean an individual who is isolated and thinks only of self but instead starts from the whole nature and character of a human being determined by their existence in society.

Methodological individualism, which originates from individualism, first takes a position to describe a group by the attributes of individual and individual as the subject to maximize utility. Second, it is the epistemology that is contrary to the sociological collectivism and the holism that pursues the theory of organism and chemismus, including functionalism.

Methodological individualism also emphasizes that only facts about individuals can ultimately explain social phenomena. Therefore, the law of large-scale social phenomena can be accepted as an explanatory premise, only if it is something that can be used as a macro law on personal facts through composition law or correspondence rule that relates individuals to large-scale phenomena. This fact is that individuals are essential elements in methodological individualism, which is the following when looking at the attributes of individuals who are subject to methodological individualism.

Individuals in Methodological Individualism

In methodological individualism, an individual is considered to be an independent decision-maker. When faced with opportunities and possibilities in the world of events, individuals pursue related interests within the strategic opportunities provided by various decision-making laws and decision-making mechanisms. Therefore, the outcome of the action is evaluated by whether or not the output is consistent with the efficiency's criterion. If so, then this raises the question of what assumptions each individual can meet the efficiency criteria.

Methodological individualism suggests that individuals become representative individuals through procedural assumptions, giving assumptions about human behavior:

First, the individual is assumed to be self-interested. The assumption that he is self-interested means that he has his preference that primarily affects the decisions he makes. However, these preferences vary from individual to individual.

Second, the individual is assumed to be rational. The meaning of rationality here is the transitive manner, which means the ability to assign sequences to all useful alternatives known to the individual.

Third, the individual is assumed to adopt a maximizing strategy. A maximization strategy is a strategy that provides the highest net profit in the light of individual preference.

Fourth, individuals are assumed to make decisions according to the level of information given to them. The level of information given to individuals is divided into the level of certainty, level of risk level, and level of uncertainty as an environmental situation surrounding decision making. At this time, it is most difficult for each individual to adopt a maximization strategy at the level of uncertainty. Individuals, however, can eventually choose a variety of strategies by reducing the means of uncertainty.

Methodological individualism, assuming a rational decision-maker as a representative individual, carries out the following roles and functions in the real world of public choice theory.

First, decision-making made by individuals is not determined solely by the individual's simple preference. In other words, public choice theory only creates rational decision-making because structured perception or motive also does rational decision-making.

Second, the outcome of decisions made within the various institutional arrangements is assessed according to how they affect individual citizens. Therefore, it is not evaluated as to how it affects groups such as society or the state, which are aggregate concepts. In this regard, methodological individualism places emphasis on the individual' role as an object by considering that a collective entity such as a state is merely a means of providing utility to an individual.

■ Basic Assumptions of Public Choice Theory

The basic assumptions that public choice theory builds are as follows.

First, the assumption in the public choice theory is that an individual will try to enjoy public goods at a minimum cost. So individuals will not be willing to volunteer for the supply and improvement of common goods and services. At the same time, they are not assumed to form an organization to pursue public interest voluntarily.

Second, it is assumed that the efficient supply and production of public goods can be possible through the establishment of institutional devices. The institutional device, which means, is a set of rules that affect the behavior of people who participate in the production and consumption of goods and services that is decision-making. Therefore, the traditional government bureaucracy organization cannot be regarded as a desirable institutional device for the supply and production of public services, so it is necessary to establish a decentralized and diverse institutional apparatus following the level of government.

3.1.3 The Relevance of Public Choice Theory

1) The Critique of Public Choice Theory

Although the public choice theory faces some criticisms for failing to reach the perfect stage as a paradigm meant by Thomas Samuel Kuhn, the substance of such criticism is not a big problem, either. However, the main criticism of the public choice theory is that it excludes human irrational aspects and experiences by overemphasizing economic rationality. This view has dramatically undermined the validity of the theoretical proposition, and the criticism is listed as follows.

First, it is a criticism of rational aspects. The instrumental rationality inherent in individualism must not be feasible in real political situations. It is pointed out that the assumption to equate the private market situation with the political situation, especially with instrumental rationality, is contradictory.

Public choice theory, for example, considers the real world to be composed of individuals who seek utility maximization. As a result, the public choice theory does not consider human values or individual freedom, but the only economical choice is considered.

Second, it is a criticism imposed by a group of political scholars who feel responsible for the political and constitutional crisis due to specific discussions on the political situation. For example, the relation model between voters and politics is not so simple as public choice theorists assume, and the hypothesis extracted from the principles they propose is not a very consistent and cohesive methodological tool. As a result, the criticism that the model presented in the public choice theory still has little empirical evidence to be supported.

Third, the public choice theory to introduce free-market logic into the public sector has its inherent limitations of market failure. The logic of the competitive market has long been criticized because it is obsessed with maintaining the status quo and the theory of balance. Therefore, the prescription of public choice theory based on the logic of the competitive market is criticized for not being relevant.

However, there is room for refutation on the issue of rationality amid such criticism. It should take into account the fact that the concept of rationality itself implies many aspects, and that its identity is ambiguous, and that misunderstanding of this concept is a phenomenon that may result from differences in perceptions between political scientists and economists. Then, the notion of rationality assumed by the public choice theory cannot be regarded as being set incorrectly.

In particular, the reason why the possibility of application is low due to lack of empirical evidence is that the spread of axiom developed in economics is short in history, not the principle of constitutionalism, which is the result of the application of the axiom developed in the realm of political philosophy.

In short, the public choice theory has been developed from the application of axiom developed in economics to fully secure basic human rights by improving imperfections in institutional devices that constitutionalism had not predicted. Besides, in the context of political philosophy, paradigmatic meaning can be found in reviving the ideological principle of contract theory, which aims to protect citizens from the abuse of power.

2) The Applicability of Public Choice Theory

The public choice theory started with the basic assumption of methodological individualism and economic rationality. As a result, it provided empirical and normative explanations for efficient supply of public goods and public services and enabled the realization of democratic administration and the efficiency of resource allocation by improving the decentralization, resilience, and responsiveness of administration.

In this context, the public choice theory provides some implications, especially in the study of public administration.

First, according to the progress of democratization and the implementation of local autonomy, the perception of individuals as analytical units has changed significantly. As a result, there will be an increase in the movement to grasp the administrative demands for individual residents. Primarily, since the local autonomy was implemented, not only the election is frequently implemented, but also in the light of the equivalence of the votes, the maximization of voting by politicians aiming for election will further increase their interest in individuals as voters.

Second, as residents' interest in the area is increasing due to the implementation of local autonomy, the perception of local public goods is changing. As a result, there will be a big problem with the externality treatment of public services. Today, the NIMBY phenomenon related to garbage and industrial waste disposal is appearing in various places, and this phenomenon is expected to accelerate further. As a way to solve this problem, negotiations between local governments and the wide-unit provision of specific services are likely to become significant issues in administrative research.

Third, much collective decision-making has been made unreasonably under the name of democracy in our society. So far, it seems that citizens were relatively indifferent to the logical basis of such collective decision-making. However, as local autonomy has been implemented, and democratization has progressed, and citizens' participation has increased, many elections and votings have been held to ensure representation.

Accordingly, the interest in rational collective decision-making rules will increase. Since choosing the right decision rule means that it has secured important public goods, it will become a major task in future administrative research.

Fourth, Public choice theory is useful in understanding the method of reasoning about administrative phenomena because it takes the deductive and legal explanation method. Thus, the public choice theory can provide empirical and prescriptive explanations of administration so that it will help with administrative theory and complementary interpretations of practice. Also, the public choice theory provides a somewhat less rigorous theory of administrative behavior than the traditional concept of public goods.

As shown above, there is a question of whether public choice theory based on the individual concept and contract theory can be accommodated in political and administrative culture with affection-centered, dogmatic, value-oriented social and cultural tradition like ours.

However, considering that our political and administrative culture is gradually shifting from a collectivistic Confucian culture to a Western pluralistic individualistic culture, the role of public choice theory will be increased as a paradigm for understanding our political and administrative phenomenon in the future.

In the end, public choice theory can be regarded as an empirical field for the improvement of institutional devices expose by constitutionalism, despite various criticisms. The public choice theory in political constructs is significant in that it emphasized that individuals, as individuals, not as aggregates like a state, should be units of analysis, and contributed to securing natural rights.

Chapter Ⅵ

Public Administration in the Neo-Conservatism and Anti-Conservatism Period

1. The Story of the Public Administration in the Neo-Conservatism and Anti-Conservatism Period

It was the discussion of government failure that began to be talked about in the government domain as the 1970s passed, such as the whirlpool. In other words, by the late 1970s, neo-conservatism or neo-liberalism, set against the backdrop of severe resource shortages and financial crises, began to spread the theory of reduction management and deregulation based on the ideology of a small government in the American administration.

The new reforms following the political and economic conservative stream called so-called Reaganomics, are beginning to focus on privatization and deregulation of government functions. Besides, the new federalism policy that increases the roles and responsibilities of the state and local governments, rather than reducing the role of the federal government, has led to the need to re-establish relations between governments from a new perspective.

With this kind of environmental change that began in the 1980s, the American administration began to focus its primary focus on privatization and reduction management, intergovernmental relations, and new personnel policy from a different perspective than in the past. As a result, theoretical discussions on public servants' reduction, government expenditure reduction, deregulation, and privatization to implement a small government were actively developed.

Of them, interest in privatization became an opportunity to recall the similarities and differences between administration and management, which were long-standing themes of public administration. Accordingly, this led to the crisis of public administration in the 1960s, which was brought up by interactions between the market and the government, once again in a situation where the boundaries became blurred.

In this regard, the first scholar to raise the argument that management and administration are all alike in trivial aspects was Wallace S. Sayre. Also, the scholar who rebelled against it was Graham T. Allison, Jr. of Harvard University.

G. T. Allison, Jr. questioned W. S. Sayre's claim and refuted W. S. Sayre's claim. G. T. Allison, Jr. also acknowledges that there is not much difference between the private and public sectors and that there is an increasing interaction between public sector managers and private sector managers. However, he emphasized that there was a fundamental difference in the perception of the top management in the two fields.

Besides, in terms of privatization and reduction management, Aron B. Wildavsky published *How to Limit Government Spending* in 1980, and Emdmuel S. Savas published *Privatizing the Public Sector* in 1982. They represent this period in that they emphasized the need to curb the growth of the government sector and promote privatization. Moreover, this trend of privatization is significant in that it became a catalyst for the reinvented government movement that swept through the 1990s.

The main area of study of administration that also flourished in this period is the intergovernmental relations. As the responsibility and role of the state and local governments due to neo-Federalism were emphasized, the scholar who laid the groundwork for a new relationship between the central and local governments, that is, the research between the governments, was Deil S. Wright.

Through his publication of *Understanding Intergovernmental Relations*, he saw the 1960s and 1970s as a time of intense competition and conflict between policies and programs. As a result of these conflicts, in the 1980s, state and local governments began to design strategies against the federal fiscal pressures, resulting in weakening trust in the federal government causing the federal government's support to decline again.

In the field of human resources administration, there is a study by Samuel Krislov, who expanded the concept of representative bureaucracy advocated by J. Donald Kingsley. The main concern of S. Krislov was on how bureaucracy could have legitimacy and public confidence if it did not represent every part of society. Since then, the representative bureaucracy that he has proposed has made a significant contribution to citizen participation, precise understanding of the goal of an action, and equal employment opportunities in the process of establishing representative bureaucracy.

Another remarkable trend In the field of human resources administration has begun to increase the distrust of public officials' ability to solve public problems. As a result, it is also a feature of this period that techniques for measuring the productivity of public officials have begun to be developed.

Besides, amid the increasing role of the government and the increasing influence and intensity of administration on the individual's life, the increasing distrust of the government and career civil service has heightened interest in administrative ethics and accountability of administration. Therefore, in 1985, the American Society for Public Administration established the Ethics Charter for Public Officials, the recent literature on public administration still shows a keen interest in the issue of administrative ethics.

As such, in the 1980s, professionalism and administrative ethics began to be perceived as a critical device for securing accountability for career civil servants. In line with this atmosphere, the Carter and Reagan administration began to reduce the discretion of career civil servants and employed strategies to increase the number of political appointees relatively.

Meanwhile, in 1979, William G. Scott and David K. Hart's *Organizational American* and in 1981,' Robert B. Denhardt's *In the Shadow of Organization* was published. Based on neo-Marxist views, they presented critical research and reform measures on bureaucracy, especially self-reflection, self-consciousness, personal communication, and face-to-face contact as channels for bureaucratic innovation.

Also, Michael M. Harmon, who advocated the action theory, criticized the existing administrative theory through the *Action Theory for Public Administration*, published in 1981. He proposed, as a new alternative, to deal with administration from the standpoint of interpretative sociology, phenomenology, symbolic interactionism, and anti-positivism. In particular, he emphasized normative theories such as interdependence, justice, and equity, and suggested administrative values such as accountability, responsiveness, and participation as new values that the administration should pursue.

Due to the wave of neo-conservatism, which began to accelerate further over the mid-1980s, the American administration began to emphasize managerial aspects of administration more than ever before. As a result, the new public management theory has emerged as a new approach to public administration, with the re-emergence of the politics-administration dichotomy, which has been quiet for a while.

The Carter administration has already initiated government reform based on the new public management that aimed at improving administrative performance by incorporating the logic and techniques of corporate management into administration. In particular, following the revision of *The Civil Service Reform Act* in 1978, the Carter administration reformed the civil service system from the viewpoint of the new public management theory, established a senior executive service, introduced a new performance evaluation system and a performance-based pay system.

The pace of new public management-based government reform began to accelerate further as it entered the Reagan administration. The Grace Commission, named as *The President's Private Sector Survey on Costs Control*, assessed the government sector as overly inefficient compared to the private sector and emphasized the improvement of efficiency through the introduction of management methods in the private sector.

The commission strongly advocated privatization and deregulation, while proposing a businesslike approach to administrative management. They also demanded that the private sector play an active role in fulfilling the demand for public services, and emphasized the increase in the beneficiary charge.

The new theoretical trends in the field of personnel administration, which began in the late 1980s, were also one of the meaningful changes. Since the 1980s, as the distrust of the administration and the career civil service system has increased, the introduction of the spoils system-centered elements has been continuously expanded. As a reaction to this, the refounding movement, which advocates the career civil service system, has emerged from the late 1980s to the early 1990s.

In this regard, James H. Svara defended the active role of public officials in the policy process by reinterpreting the existing politics-administration dichotomy. In other words, the four functions of mission, policy, administration, and management are required to implement an effective government. However, J. H. Svara claims that in the process of establishing the mission of the government, the existing politics-administration dichotomy has made the mistake of dealing with only the relationship between policy and administration while overlooking the role of the career civil servants.

Gary L. Wormsley also supported the refounding movement through the writings of the *Refounding Public Administration* in 1990, and Larry D. Terry and Charles T. Goodsell also played a significant role in such movements. The advocates of the refounding movement have warned against the expansion of spoils system based appointments while defending the career civil service system and calling for rediscovering rather than reinventing the government.

However, shortly after the publication of works related to the refounding movement, David Osborne and Ted Gabeler argued that the government should instead be reinvented through the joint-authors *Reinventing Government.* They also stressed the need to rebuild the government and that the private sector needs to take part in the supply of public services.

Their arguments later provided the theoretical basis for the reinventing government movement, which was initiated by the National Performance Review, which was formed by Vice President Al Gore as part of reform strategy of the federal government in the Clinton administration.

The reinventing government movement, led by the Clinton administration, was to apply the new public management theory to administrative reform. However, with the spread of the reinventing government movement in the 1990s, there has been a continuous debate in the United States about the relevance of the private sector' role in providing public services, along with the question of the desirability of the movement. As such, since the mid-1980s, deregulation, and privatization have been widespread, gradually destroying the monopolies of the government sector. Now, the government has to compete on an equal footing with the private and social sectors as a single competitor in the supply of public services.

In response to changes in the status and role of government as a competitor, in the 1990s, a new trend of research on the customer-driven administration and search for "who is administration for?" began to be formed. Besides, with greater private sector involvement in the supply of public services and the emergence of a new public service delivery system, research on new governance to deal with these issues has also begun to thrive.

The wave of neo-liberalism and globalization that began to flourish around the world came as a massive storm to American administrative theory. This vast wave was that it should satisfy the high-quality needs of citizens and not shy away from competition in good faith with leading private companies.

Meanwhile, the conservatism-oriented of the administration, which had come up like a massive storm, faced an unexpected environment as it entered the 2000s. The first is the change of perspective on the new public management theory, which has played a leading role in conservatism. Second is the financial crisis following Lehman Brothers' bankruptcy in 2008.

As a reform model based on the new public management theory became established in the Clinton administration, a group of public administration scholars began rebelling against this trend since the mid-1990s. For example, in 1996, the American Society for Public Administration emphasized publicness as a new role in the administration, with criticism of the falsity of the new public management model.

Led by Horace G. Frederickson, these discussions have begun to be featured in the *American Public Administration Review*. Later, in-depth discussions began to take place on the search for the role of the administration that could not be replaced by the role of the market and on the differences between the public and market sector.

Nevertheless, it is hard to say that the American administrative theory of the 2000s is entirely free from the neoliberal wave. While many public administration scholars, including H. G. Frederickson, emphasize the specificity of administration differentiated from management, the wave of market-oriented and business-oriented management trends is deeply ingrained in the development process of American administrative theory.

Besides, the market failure following the collapse of Lehman Brothers in 2008 calls for a new prescription in a different context. In other words, new market failure has resulted in legitimacy for reinforcement of government regulations on markets. Also, the government's ever-worsening fiscal deficit serves as an opportunity to strengthen the so-called anti-conservative policy orientation, which requires the revision of conservative fiscal policies centered on the existing tax cuts policy.

In addition, the government's interventionism is intensifying, as seen in the Obama administration, especially in the reform plan for compulsory health insurance, giving a glimpse of its anti-conservative policy orientation. However, what is interesting in this process is that as the resistance to the government's interventionism is strengthened, the concept of libertarian paternalism is spreading to alleviate the side effects and to emphasize the legitimacy of the government's interventionism.

This interventionism is the concept that Richard H. Thaler and Cass R. Sunstein argue based on behavioral economics. If the existing government interventionism was a concept that excluded freedom of choice, liberal interventionism reflects the freedom of choice boldly on the contrary.

According to them, the way to relieve the inconveniences of government interventionism is to divine-human behavior and to make the right decisions by nudging in their sides. Liberal interventionism is a concept that is emphasized mainly in the field of economic policy in order to overcome the limitation of government interventionism. However, this concept is criticized in that it overlooks the fact that it can still promote uniformity by creating unnecessary coercion on the free choice of a human being.

Meanwhile, another trend to be examined in the context of anti-conservative policy orientation is the reinforcement of neo-protectionism. This neo-protectionism can be said to be developed country-centered protectionism that emerged as developed countries such as the United States stepped up regulations on trade and foreign currency in order to cope with new market failures caused by globalization.

In other words, neo-protectionism emerged to prevent the economic recession of the United States caused by the collapse of the Bretton Woods System, the oil shock and chronic deficit in the international balance of payments.

In the United States, however, neo-protectionism is not a recent policy trend. Neo-protectionism has already begun since the so-called 'Buy American' clause was tightened to mandate the use of only U.S.-made products for large-scale public works projects in the United States to stimulate the economy. Besides, by strengthening the neo-protectionism to protect its economy in the Trump administration, the world is returning to protectionism in the 19th century instead of globalization based on free trade.

The myth of globalization, which has been the belief that the world is bound together as an economic bloc, is doomed to be abandoned. Accordingly, the new international order leading to the strengthening of neo-protectionism requires a new administrative paradigm that is far different from the one when neo-liberalism dominated. As such, from the 1980s to the present, the American administrative theory has been reversed from the conservative wave to anti-conservative again.

2. The Representative Scholars in the Neo-Conservatism and Anti-Conservatism Period

From the 1980s to the present, the characteristics of American administrative theory have tended to shift from conservative waves to anti-conservative. The characteristics of the development process of administrative theory in this period are as follows from the standpoint of representative scholars.

2.1 Emanuel S. Savas's Privatization

The 1980s was a time when reduction management became a trend, along with the decline in the role of the government sector. At this time, Emanuel S. Savas wrote the *Privatizing The Public Sector: How to Shrink Government* in 1982 and *Privatization: The Key to Better Government* in 1987. In these two books, he argued for the privatization of government services, a trend of the times.

Along with the recognition of the need for privatization, E. S. Savas approached the need for privatization from a new perspective: division of roles between the private and government sectors. According to him, privatization was considered to reduce the scope of the government and increase the scope of the private sector in the provision of public services or ownership of a property for them. In other words, E. S. Savas saw reducing the government's burden by leaving the production area of goods and services to the private sector as privatization.

In this regard, E. S. Savas cites the following background for the need for privatization:

First, there is a practical need for privatization. This need is because the government can save and streamline the provision of public services through prudent privatization. Thus, privatization can contribute to the realization of a better government.

Second, there is a need for an ideological side called a small government. The current government is already so big and powerful that it is feared to infringe on the privacy of its people, hampering the realization of democracy. As a result, the decision of the big government is originally political, and it is considered to be less valid than the decisions made in the equal relationship among individuals.

Third, there is a need in terms of commercialism. This need is a benefit to the private sector in that the private sector can do more business management by reducing the area of government.

Fourth, the populists claim that they are making a better society. They argue that when deciding on public services, residents should have more comprehensive decision-making power. For example, community organizations such as families and charities close to the residents rather than by government bureaucracies should supply public services.

In conclusion, in support of privatization, E. S. Savas maintains that reducing the size of the government and increasing the role of the private sector based on incentives and competition are desirable for a better society. As mentioned by the reason for expanding privatization, some public services in society can only be provided through collective decision-making processes, but many services can be provided without going through these processes.

In other words, the provision of large-scale services can only be achieved through the government, but it can also be done through voluntary agencies in small cases. Therefore, since expanding the scope of government could impede the supply of these voluntary public services, it is a critical factor in the E. S. Savas's argument that the production of public goods in government, which is not based on the principle of competition, maybe inferior to that of the private sector.

2.2 Deil S. Wright's Intergovernmental Relations

While traditional administrative theories have primarily focused on phenomena such as the organization and composition of the central government, personnel, and finance, and policy-making processes, the Deil S. Wright's intergovernmental relations(IGR) have contributed to the attention to the regional and local government issues that have been neglected in the past.

D. S. Wright's interest was in establishing an analytical framework that would systematically explain the intergovernmental relations at different levels in this context. D. S. Wright's intergovernmental relationships are a conceptual framework for explaining the nature and operational characteristics of the structure and function of the federal system of the American government, which differs in many respects from conventional federalism. D. S. Wright's discussion began by describing the difference between intergovernmental relations and federalism.

According to D. S. Wright, the intergovernmental relationships are not a mere term replacing federalism, but rather a term that deals with a series of phenomena and behaviors that are not included in federalism. Thus, the intergovernmental relationships do not deal only with the relationship between the federal government and the state, but rather deal with a wide range of policy tasks instead of assuming hierarchical relations between each government.

That is why intergovernmental relations are a much more neutral concept than federalism. D. S. Wright argued the following differences between federalism and intergovernmental relations. So the intergovernmental relationship is a far more neutral concept than federalism. D. S. Wright insisted on the difference between federalism and intergovernmental relations:

First, federalism has historically emphasized the relationships between federal and state governments. Intergovernmental relations, on the other hand, focus on analyzing interactions between governments in all forms and levels.

Second, federalism has been mostly dependent on legal approaches such as legal authority and official behavior. Intergovernmental relations, on the other hand, give more attention to informal, invisible acts, activities, and the perception of actors beyond the legal focus.

Third, federalism is a theory based on hierarchical power relationships, whereas intergovernmental relations do not assume up-and-down relations according to authority relations between various governments. In other words, it means approaching each government from a horizontal perspective.

Fourth, federalism does not place much weight on policy issues. On the other hand, intergovernmental relations have a great interest in the way policies formed and implemented between governments and what the consequences will be.

Fifth, federalism has long been abused by users with different political goals, reducing the analytical utility of the concept. On the other hand, the intergovernmental relations have a neutral nature as a concept with a more restrictive and strict meaning, so there is a discrimination in that it does not contain any emotional meaning.

D. S. Wright's emphasis on intergovernmental relations does not seem to be in the pursuit of establishing an independent theoretical framework. Instead, it focuses more on analyzing and describing the operational aspects that take place in various governments. Therefore, D. S. Wright's intergovernmental relations are meaningful in that it presents a topic to be explored rather than value as an analysis framework. However, D. S. Wright's intergovernmental relations are doubtful to be applied in the case of the non-federal state form, and there is also a problem in the sophistication of the contents.

2.3 Charles T. Goodsell's Bureaucracy Advocacy

Charles T. Goodsell defended the American government bureaucracy with a considerable persuasive and systematic approach to the criticism imposed on the bureaucracy through the publication of *The Case for Bureaucracy: A Public Administration Polemic* in

1985. C. T. Goodsell's advocacy for bureaucracy proceeded in three orders. First, he collected and arranged the criticisms that have been made up to now on the bureaucracy. Second, he sought to highlight the positive side of the bureaucracy through re-criticism from the theoretical and empirical viewpoints on these criticisms. Third, he conducted the study by tracing why the bureaucracy was nonetheless negatively illuminated.

C. T. Goodsell has sorted out the elements of criticism being imposed on bureaucracy into low performance, power-oriented, and loss of humanity. So he attempted to re-criticize the criticism being imposed on the bureaucracy as follows.

First, it is a re-criticism against the criticism that is being imposed on the low performance of bureaucracy. He pointed out that economists' argument that government bureaucracy is inefficient is a severe problem, even though contradictory evidence exists at the same time, to make deductive reasoning in the way that the bureaucracy is inferior in any way. In addition, he also countered that while sociologists are particularly critical of the dysfunctional aspect of bureaucracy, this is a mistake caused by excessive simplification.

Second, it is a re-criticism against the criticism that is being imposed on the excessive power orientation of bureaucracy. Although bureaucracy exists for the benefit of the vested interests, it is not organized for their benefit. In particular, the fact that the government officials' policy-oriented attitude makes little difference from the general public is an example that reflects this. Moreover, he pointed out the bureaucracy has functionally represented the interests of the general public.

In other words, he stressed that while inequality in American society has existed and still exists today, it is either a sin held by the whole society or a legacy of history and that the toxic bureaucracy is not the only reason to be criticized. On the contrary, C. T. Goodsell stressed that the bureaucracy was organized to solve the economic inequalities that arise when left to a market economy, and argued that it is more appropriate for the bureaucracy to work for it.

Third, it is a re-criticism against the criticism that is being imposed on the loss of human nature of bureaucracy. Although there is a different bureaucratic character, the survey shows that bureaucrats do not have a completely different personality from ordinary citizens. In particular, he refuted that the bureaucrats treat customers with rules and impersonality, which is not true either.

In the end, even though the fact that the government bureaucracy is satisfactory, his principal argument is that the reason for the negative understanding of the bureaucracy is the gap between the actual and abstract images. In other words, he believes that this interval has taken place in a kind of myth. American society has a myth that has solved all the problems for a long time, and it continued to have an optimistic belief that it could be solved.

However, if the goal set in this atmosphere is not achieved, they think something is wrong, and this gap has occurred in trying to find the mistake in the bureaucracy. Also, C. T. Goodsell pointed out that the myth of lousy bureaucracy was expanded and reproduced in the course of contact with the government bureaucracy, with excuses from those who did not achieve their personal goals.

As a result, C. T. Goodsell is in the position that the academic world must understand the government bureaucracy and actively advocate it, as a criticism of the government bureaucracy has lost its sense of balance. So, he emphasized the importance of balanced media coverage and the need to increase the area of direct contact so that the gap between government bureaucracies does not occur. Finally, C. T. Goodsell's advocacy for bureaucracy can be found in terms of suggesting a balanced discourse on bureaucracy, which is based on a negative perspective.

2.4 David Osborne and Ted Gaebler's Reinventing Government

David Osborne and Ted Gaebler co-authored the *Reinventing Government: How the Entrepreneurial Spirit Transforming the Public Sector* in 1992 had a profound impact on American government reforms that have been undergoing a wave of neo-conservatism since the 1990s.

In particular, Osborne is a member of the National Academy of Sciences and the Progressive Policy Institute, the composition of the reinventing government task force run by Vice President Al Gore, and has led government innovation through the entrepreneurship.

2.4.1 The Characteristics of Entrepreneurial Approach

D. Osborne proposed a new type of governance, called an entrepreneurial approach, rather than a bureaucratic approach to administration. D. Osborne emphasized that the differentiation of an entrepreneurial approach as new governance should change the mindset and behavior of bureaucrats.

First, in terms of the government's new role, the government should steer rather than rowing, as it has traditionally been.

Second, in terms of the government's activities, the government should be shifted to empowering bureaucrats rather than providing services as usual.

Third, in terms of the supply of services, the government should introduce the concept of competition in the provision of services rather than the monopoly of services as it has traditionally been.

Fourth, in terms of management style, the government should shift from rule-centered or role-based to mission-oriented, as it has traditionally been.

Fifth, in terms of the budget system, the government should change from the past input-oriented budget system to the budget allocation method linked to performance.

Sixth, in terms of administrative value, the government should shift from a bureaucracy-centered like the past to a customer-oriented one.

Seventh, in terms of the purpose of the budget, the government should shift from the past spending-oriented method to profit-making.

Eighth, in terms of government action, the government should change from a traditional treatment-oriented government to a preventive one.

Ninth, in terms of the composition of the system, the government should shift from a hierarchical organization like the past to a system that values teamwork and participation.

Tenth, in terms of operating mechanisms, the government should transform itself from an organizational-oriented like the past to a market-oriented.

Finally, in terms of administrative style, the government should shift from command and control centered like the past to administrative mode through consultation and network formation.

2.4.2 New Government Forms by Market-Oriented Approach

D. Osborne insisted that the government should be transformed into a new form through market-oriented reforms, as he argued for.

First, it should be a catalytic government that focuses more on policy coordination than policy implementation. A catalytic government means a small but strong government. So, the facilitative government does not work less but instead refers to a government that takes charge of more policies for the community and moves the system.

Second, the community-owned government should be created. Community-owned government means a government that devotes more authority to residents than a government that focuses on providing services to residents because community organizations have more interest in community development than anyone else. Therefore, this interest tries to solve many problems affecting their lives on their own, which could soon hasten the realization of participatory democracy. In this regard, the community-owned government aims at the value of participatory democracy.

Third, a competitive government should be established. This competitive government means that when delivering government services, the government should introduce a competition system away from its monopolistic methods, such as in the past.

Fourth, the mission-driven government should be created. This means that it should be reborn as a mission-oriented organization, not a government that is centered on rules or regulations. Such a government is intended to ease regulations within the bureaucracy by removing internal rules and simplifying the administrative system. Therefore, the success of a mission-driven government depends on how they develop and combine the mission-driven budget system and performance measurement system.

Fifth, it should be directed toward a result-oriented government. Whether or not the government composed of bureaucracy achieves its goals is only possible through accurate performance measures. To this end, it is necessary to develop measurement tools to measure the performance of bureaucracy.

Sixth, the customer-driven government should be established. Customer-driven government is non-political and meaningful to stimulate innovation. Accordingly, the customer-driven government should reduce wastage, encourage customer participation, and create a broader range of equal opportunities so that customers can choose the service they want.

Seventh, it should be directed toward an entrepreneurial government. An entrepreneurial government means a government that emphasizes income rather than an expenditure. In this sense, an entrepreneurial government is not a government to make money, but to weigh the investment value of a project to save money.

Eighth, it should be an anticipatory government. An anticipatory government means the government to prevent problems in advance, rather than delivering services to correct them after problems occur. It is necessary to prepare incentives to change the behavior of policymakers to build a government to prepare for the future. For example, in an entrepreneurial government, efforts should be made to change incentives through changes in the budget system, changes in the accounting system, administration over regional boundaries, and reform of the electoral system.

Ninth, a decentralized government should be established. A decentralized government is a government that attaches more importance to participation and teamwork than hierarchy, which has transferred the authority to allow civil servants who face customers face-to-face to make decisions. As a result, decentralized governments are more flexible than centralized governments, and can respond to changing environments and consumer needs. Besides, the decentralized government has a task-oriented nature, which is meaningful in that task-oriented government can cope well with complex and changing environments.

Tenth, the market-oriented government should be built. This means a government that solves problems by utilizing the private sector's market rather than using administrative mechanisms such as direct delivery of services, orders, and control regulations to solve the problem.

As mentioned above, D. Osborne's market–oriented government model has had a profound impact on the reform direction of the Clinton administration in particular. However, D. Osborne's market-oriented government model has resulted in disparaging or degrading of the government's objectives by oversimplifying or neglecting the differences between the market and the government. As a result, from the mid-1990s, market-oriented models of government have faced intense criticism since the mid-1990s.

2.5 Richard Thaler and Cass R. Sunstein's Libertarian Paternalism

The bankruptcy of Lehman Brothers, which hit the American economy in 2008 with the retrogression of liberalistic waves, has been a decisive moment to change the market's superior view of the government. The so-called new market failure facing the American economy and administration has once again given legitimacy to the government's paternalism of tightening government regulations. Also, the debate over the government's interventionism is raging over the Obama administration's reform plan for compulsory health insurance.

However, the core of the resistance to the government's paternalism is that it runs counter to the underlying belief of liberalism that the individual's choice should be respected as much as possible unless the individual's choice is contrary to the interests of others. Accordingly, what appeared to alleviate the side effects of the government's paternalism and at the same time emphasize the legitimacy of government's paternalism is the libertarian paternalism as the social philosophy pursued by behavioral economics.

Richard H. Thaler and Cass R. Sunstein make the following assumptions to develop the concept of libertarian paternalism: That is, the reason why individuals do not make desirable choices is that they have not enough information and self-control ability to make a reasonable judgment. Therefore, libertarian paternalism is the view to influence personal choice by providing sufficient information and environment for individuals to make desirable decisions.

Libertarian paternalism maintains ethically conservative stance, while philosophically espousing liberalism. Accordingly, libertarian paternalism is based on the liberal philosophy of John S. Mill and such concepts as the limited rationality of Herbert A. Simon and the assumptions of irrationality held by decision-making under the uncertainty emphasized by Daniel Kahneman & Amos Tversky.

As a result, libertarian paternalism introduces a behavioral assumption that can change human behavior through governmental information provision or indirect means of intervention instead of assuming that personal choice is reasonable. Thus, libertarian paternalism is based on human irrationality assumed by behavioral economics.

The advantage of libertarian paternalism is that it can reduce resistance and reduce policy costs, among other things, by reducing the risk of limiting the freedom of individuals that can result from direct government intervention. In particular, it is focused on the fact that by voluntarily inducing changes in individuals' behavior in the process, the government can continue to maintain the effectiveness of its policies by enhancing compliance with the policies.

However, libertarian paternalism, despite its advantages, is silent on who judges whether it is a matter of desirable choice, which is the most essential and fundamental issue. That is, there is little evidence that the government's choice is superior to the individual's choice. Thus, libertarian paternalism faces the criticism that it is nothing more than imposing government values on individuals.

In the end, libertarian paternalism can be quite dangerous, given the possibility that governments can make erroneous decisions just as individuals make wrong decisions.

3. The Representative Theory in the Neo-Conservatism and Anti-Conservatism Period

The representative administrative theories that emerged in the neo-conservatism and anti-conservatism period of public administration are new public management theory and new public service theory. The background and characteristics and contents of the theories that led to the formation of the new public management theory and the new public service theory are as follows.

3.1 New Public Management Theory

3.1.1 The Background of New Public Management Theory

The bureaucratic paradigm, which was introduced in the progressive era to secure responsibility for democratic institutions, faced the challenge of a post-bureaucratic paradigm characterized by anti-government, anti-bureaucracy, and anti-taxation from the late 1970s. As a result, the issue of whether this trend could become a new paradigm enough to replace the bureaucratic paradigm in the administration and the debate over its effectiveness and relevance accordingly has emerged as an essential issue.

The new trend raised by conservative governments and scholars based on neoliberalism has had tremendous potential for change despite the degree of weak theorization. This trend, categorized mainly as new managerialism centering around Britain and an entrepreneurial government model centering on the United States, aims to achieve the fundamental value of administration, efficiency, and responsiveness, through a similar method to competitive market mechanisms and popular approach.

The government thus faced a situation in which it had to create a new system of rewards and incentives, and give new authority to citizens and bureaucrats to pursue them. It also had to give the service recipient the choice to impose the incentive system. As a result, the focus of the new paradigm is focused on the customer-centered, result-centered, and competitive-driven government

On the practical side, meanwhile, the practitioners familiar with the market mechanism participated in the formation of theories, and the active support of the leaders needed to transform them into a reform process played an important role. For reference, OECD uses the term 'new public management' by combining neo-managerialism, post-bureaucratic paradigm, and entrepreneurial government model. The background of new public management theory is divided into the environmental and theoretical aspect as follows.

1) The Environmental Background of New Public Management Theory

The environmental factors that led to the emergence of new public management theory in countries, including the United Kingdom and the United States, are as follows.

First, in the 1970s, the burden of high welfare costs and the inefficiency of the public sector in developed countries were on the rise. As a result, voters have begun to raise active calls for reform on the fiscal deficit. In other words, the reform of the big government, which flourished until the early 1970s became the request of the times due to the slowdown in economic growth, the increase in the current account deficit, and the increase in the fiscal deficit and the cumulative debt in the public sector.

Second, the productivity of the public sector lags behind that of the private sector, as seen in the introduction of privatization and external contract systems, resulting in poor performance in the public sector. Also, the questions of the effectiveness of government intervention that the government can no longer provide solutions for all situations, and the need for new capabilities to adapt to the harsh environment have led to this model.

Third, it is a desire to strengthen national competitiveness, which is a common concern of each country by following the trend of globalization. The impact of government productivity on overall national competitiveness is substantial. Therefore, the situation of strengthening national competitiveness forced each country to introduce new public management theory.

In addition, the concerns that the public sector imposes unnecessary burdens on the private sector and hinders development, the decline in expectations for the government's ability to no longer address the economic and social problems held by the government with traditional prescriptions, the expansion of high responsiveness and choice, the increase in citizens' demand for quality of administrative services, the expansion of the desire for change of internal employees in the public sector, and the development of information technology can also be considered as environmental factors of model selection.

2) The Theoretical Background of New Public Management Theory

The theoretical foundation of the new public management theory is the neo-managerialism and economics developed in the private sector.

First, neo-managerialism, one of the theoretical foundations of the new public management theory, is used interchangeably with neo-Taylorism. This implies new trends that apply business-type managerialism to the public domain.

Second, the economics that influenced the new public management theory is mainly microeconomics(neo-institutional economics and organizational economics). These include public choice theory, principal-agent theory, and transaction cost theory. Therefore, the theoretical basis of the new public management theory can be seen as a complex mixture of managerialism, public choice theory, principal-agent theory, and transaction cost theory.

The new public management theory, which is composed of various theoretical foundations, differs slightly from the theoretical development process according to the country. For example, there is a difference between neo-managerialism centered around the United Kingdom and entrepreneurial government model developed in the United States.

However, while the reform movement based on the new public management theory differs in width, depth, and success depends on the country, but the goals and techniques pursued are similar. The core of the movement was to focus on maximizing the productivity and efficiency of non-responsive administrative organizations, which have been run by bureaucrats.

3.1.2 The Contents and characteristics of New Public Management Theory.

1) The Concept of New Public Management Theory

The new public management theory, which spread around the world as part of the government innovation movement, was first used by Christopher Hood. Since then, the OECD has defined it as an innovation that is carried out both domestically and internationally. Besides, the new public management theory is called a variety of names such as market-oriented administration, entrepreneurial government, public management, managerialism, government innovation movement, and new managerialism.

However, despite the diversity of names, the new public management theory is a movement to introduce management techniques applied to private management, such as market and competition principles to the administrative sector, which is generally agreed to value the achievement and performance of the government sector and to emphasize the personal responsibility of managers.

The new public management theory, which has constructed a new field in public administration, began to emerge through the form of the British and U.S. government reform in the 1970s and 1980s when expectations for market theory were abundant in the times. Moreover, as David Osborne and Ted Gaebler put it together convincingly in the 1990s, Vice President Al Gore reflected that argument in the report of the National Performance Review, spreading into international trends and contributing to the formation of a new paradigm.

The new public management theory is different from the reforms that have been carried out in the past in this respect. If past reforms have focused primarily on reducing costs, the new public management theory differs in that it operates with more specific programs in theory and practice.

Also, because the new public management theory tries to replace the traditional administrative model, its primary purpose is to transform the relationship between the public sector and the government and society. The appearance of reform in the public sector varies from country to country, depending on the differences in political and economic systems, and the government reform movement also differs in scope, depth, and success depends on the country.

However, what is common in the reform movements of all countries is the use of an economic market as a model for the relationship between politics and administration, and the goal of reform and the technology used are becoming similar.

2) The Types of New Public Management Theory

The new public management theory is divided into the entrepreneurial government model centered on the United States and the neo-managerialism model centered on the Commonwealth. Despite some differences in content, the aim of improving government performance and management efficiency in response to changes in the administrative environment is similar. In other words, the bureaucratic paradigm, which focuses on rules and procedures, while clinging to the mechanical efficiency summarized by monopoly, power, rigidity, and uniformity, can not cope with change.

This is similar to the post-bureaucratic paradigm proposed by Michael Barzelay. For example, in the post-bureaucratic paradigm, the new government innovation model should pursue the outcomes-oriented administration, emphasis on quality and value, restoration of organizational goals, creation of voluntary administrative responsibility, problem-solving oriented. As a result, the ultimate goal of the new public management theory can be summarized as introducing the competition-oriented, performance-oriented, and customer-oriented market model into the administration.

However, despite the nature of the new public management theory, it is not easy to characterize it in a common form because it has been developed variously by period, country, and region. Therefore, on the assumption that the form of the new public management theory is diverse, this chapter will typically focus on the form of the United Kingdom and the United States.

■ American Model

Melvin J. Dubnick, a theoretical trend that emerged as a backlash against the bureaucratic paradigm in the United States since the late 1970s, presented minimal state theory, deregulating government theory and reinventing government theory. This tendency is generally included in the category of post-bureaucratic paradigms, as shown in Table 1.

The post-bureaucratic paradigm centered on the United States is divided into three groups according to political ideology and strategic differences.

First, the minimal state theory implies that the government should limit its purpose to the supply of public goods, and it has a negative stance on the nature of the administration. For example, the minimal state theory considered the administration as a selfish pursuit of self-interest and the organization's budget maximization, although it regarded the nature of administration as reasonable. It, therefore, suggested that the administration should be transformed into a competitive organization such as the market and that the approach to this should be shifted to a cost-minimization strategy and a consumer-centered management approach.

Second, the deregulating government theory emphasizes privatization and deregulation above all else. The content of the deregulation school is summarized in its entirety in the Paul Volcker report written in 1989. This school, which has been evaluated as having built the most sophisticated theory among the three schools, has put the primary purpose of the government in solving public problems. It presented a loose hierarchy in the form of a preferred organization, with management orientation emphasizing on balance between control and flexibility from the point of view of the arbitrator.

Third, despite the weakness that the lack of theory is based on the previous two theories, the most recent reinventing government

[Table 1] Comparing the Bureaucratic Paradigm and the Post–Bureaucratic Paradigm

Characteristic	Bureaucratic Paradigm	Post–Bureaucratic Paradigm		
		Minimal State Theory	Deregulating Government Theory	Reinventing Government Theory
Purpose of government	• Enforcement of national will	• Public goods Service provision	• Solution to public problems	• Response to civic expectation
Civil servant	• Neutrality	• Rational • Maximization of interest	• Publicness	• Entrepreneur
Task organization	• Strict hierarchy	• Competitive • Market multiples organization	• Loose hierarchy	• Loose organization
Management method	• Strict supervision • Standard operating procedures	• Minimum cost • Customer–oriented management	• Mediation management • Balance and resilience	• Efficient quality management

model has the advantage of presenting vital reform measures, focusing on the experience of practitioners. The entrepreneurial government model advocated by neo-liberalists and neo-conservatives represented by David Osborne and Ted Gaebler relies on a mechanism of robust market approaches and individual choice for the provision of public services, similar to neo-managerialism. This model seeks the appropriate type of organization as the type of organization and emphasizes facilitative as the management style.

Although the new public management model that emerged in the U.S. differs slightly in terms of content, it generally works by combining the characteristics of the three models over time.

■ Commonwealth Model

The neo-managerialism developed in the Commonwealth countries centered on the United Kingdom is a trend to transplant or match a business model with embedded market individualism based on new right-wing thought to the core value of the public sector.

The neo-managerialism in the United Kingdom, which began to be strengthened in the 1990s, was evaluated as deepening the government's corporatization into more creative values, although it differed in view. The neo-managerialism focuses on the principle of public works and the recognition of customers and focuses on achieving 3E of economy, efficiency, and effectiveness, which are the main goals of organizational management.

In this regard, the neo-managerialism rejects the importance of the specialty and procedures and rules of public administration, which is the underlying assumption of traditional public administration. Instead, it argues that socio-economic problems can be cured by improved management, assuming that the management, which is an instrumental activity, can be applied to both public and private organization.

In this sense, the neo-managerialism is a management style that seeks to break away from conventional bureaucratic guardianship and pursue reorganization of the organization, decentralization, morale promotion, improvement of the compensation system, reduction management, an increase of responsiveness, and dynamics of the corporate culture. The common factors that led to the neo-managerial administrative reform in Commonwealth countries, including the United Kingdom, were as follows.

First, the budget deficit has become severe due to the economic slowdown and financial pressure.

Second, the distrust of the new right against the big government and the dwindling national boundaries have resulted in an era.

Third, there is a phenomenon of Europeanization that has brought new pressure to the administration.

Fourth, public dissatisfactions with inefficient government performance were rising.

Fifth, management trends, such as the new public management model have become popular around the world.

Sixth, the development of information technology has created a favorable environment for introducing new public management reform model.

In conclusion, the theoretical foundation for substantial government reform in the United Kingdom is rooted in managerialism and neo-institutional economics.

3) The Contents and Characteristics of New Public Management Theory

In the western capitalist societies, such as the United Kingdom and the United States, the direction of the typical change pursued by the neo-conservative government was an effort to build a belief in new governance and make the government more effective and responsive. Therefore, what is pointed out in common among the discussions on government reform based on the new public management are the pursuit of customer satisfaction, the elimination of red tape, the granting of autonomy, the reduction of costs and the pursuit of profit.

Among them, customer satisfaction means to correct the administration centered on suppliers' convenience, and removing the red tape is meaningful in overhauling various regulations and systems that have entangled public servants and citizens. Also, the granting of autonomy is meaningful in enhancing administrative excellence by improving the quality of working life that can enhance the ability of civil servants while avoiding control-oriented organizational management. Finally, it can be summarized as pursuing the consolidation of ministries and profit-making business to improve efficiency.

The new public management theory, which emerged in the late 1970s in response to the incompatibility of the traditional administrative model, alleviates the problems of the traditional bureaucratic model and means that there is a significant change in the way the public sector operates. Thus, as Christopher Hood mentioned, the background of the emergence of new public management theory is the form of response to changes in social conditions following post-industrial society and post-Fordism.

As already mentioned, not only is the new public management theory different from country, region, and age, but also its name and scope vary, making it challenging to derive characteristics. Nevertheless, the new public management theory contains common components, such as the introduction of competition principles, the delegation of authority to the front line, and management by performance. From this point of view, the characteristics of the new public management theory are as follows.

First, the new public management theory emphasizes the introduction of competition principles. To this end, it advocates the introduction of market-like mechanisms or privately developed management techniques. The introduction of competition principles is the distinctive feature that is most different from the traditional bureaucracy model to be described later.

Second, it emphasizes the delegation of powers to the front line agencies and the reduction of government functions. This means that the new public management theory focuses on the improvement of productivity through decentralization and dismantling of bureaucracy. Besides, management by performance is a characteristic element in line with the introduction of competition principles, which can also be seen as a result of counteraction to the negligence of meritocracy under the excessive input-oriented control method undertaken by the existing bureaucracy.

Another essential characteristic of the new public management theory is that it points out that the bureaucratic system has been operated with excessive rules and control, and that there is a severe problem of responding to the needs of customers who are citizens. The new public management theory raised the necessity of strengthening the power of citizen as a customer.

As described above, the characteristic elements of the new public management theory are compared with those of the traditional administrative theory, which is the same as Table 2. As shown in Table 2, new public management theory pursues businessman based on economic theory, unlike traditional administrative theory. Thus, the traditional administrative theory focuses on voters, while the new public management theory relies on the corporate view of customers.

Accordingly, the role of the government emphasizes not as a policy-making or executive function based on a politically deter

[Table 2] Comparison of Traditional Administrative Theory and New Public Management Theory

Perspective \ Type	Traditional administrative theory	New public management theory
Foundation of theory and recognition	• Early Social Science	• Economic theory • Sophisticated discussion–based on positive social science
Rationality model and behavioral model	• General rationality • Administrator	• Technical and economic rationality • Economic man or decision–makers based on self–interest
Position on public interest	• Political decisions expressed by law	• Gross profits of individuals
Bureaucrat's reaction target	• Customers and voters	• Customers
Role of government	• Rowing (policy formulation and enforcement focused on a single, politically determined goal)	• Direction (Catalyst utilizing market power)
Mechanism of achieving policy goals	• Programs through existing governmental organizations	• Create mechanisms and incentives to achieve policy goals by utilizing individuals and nonprofit organizations
Responsibility approach	• Hierarchies–administrators respond to democratically elected political leaders	• Market–oriented–totaling personal interests create desirable outcomes for citizens or customer groups
Administrative discretion	• Allow only limited discretion to bureaucrats	• Allow broad discretion to achieve corporate objectives
Expected organizational structure	• Regulation and control of bureaucratic organization and customers moving under the supervision of the government	• Decentralized public institutions that perform basic controls
Motivation of bureaucracy	• Wages and benefits • Public employee protection	• Entrepreneurship • Ideological desire to reduce the size of the government

mined goal but direction-taking as a catalyst using the power of the market. Besides, the mechanism for achieving policy goals also emphasizes the importance of incentive systems, not just government agencies.

Even in the matter of responsibility and discretion, the new public management theory is not responsible for political leaders but is determined by how much favorable results are generated for customers, and for this, a broad discretion and decentralized organization should be given. In particular, the motivation for creating desirable results should also be expressed in the entrepreneurial spirit.

The characteristics of the new public management theory challenge the underlying assumption that the traditional government model has pursued, provided that the traditional administrative model did not work efficiently. As a result, the new public management theory prefers economists and management trainees rather than typical administrators, introduces management techniques from the private sector, breaks the boundaries of the public and private sectors to reduce costs, and changes working conditions within a system that is no longer needed to increase the productivity of the government. In conclusion, the characteristics of the new public management theory can be summarized as follows.

First, it uses market-like mechanisms such as the introduction of competition principles, the introduction of private management techniques, and privatization.

Second, it seeks to replace the existing hierarchical bureaucracy through a decentralization strategy such as devolution of authority or granting administrative flexibility.

Third, it aims toward consumer-centric that is responsive to the needs of customers using administrative services, emphasizing performance-oriented, and quality improvement.

3.1.3 The Relevance of New Public Management Theory

1) The Critique of New Public Management Theory

The new public management theory, which has been developed based on Western cultures such as the United Kingdom and the United States, is also heating the debate over the relevance and effectiveness of the model, despite its positive factors and contributions.

From the viewpoint of active acceptance to the new public management theory to critical acceptance, the spectrum is diverse. Here, from the viewpoint of the relevance of the model, the following is examined.

■ The Relevance in Political Philosophy

From the political-philosophical point of view, the question is, among other things, whether the market model claimed by the new public management theory is compatible with democratic values. If the administration system that should realize democratic values introduce the method used in the enterprise, it is criticized that it does not solve the problem but rather causes another problem and there is little possibility of compatible with the value pursued by the administration.

Also, if the administration excessively prefers the corporate management method, the administration could be separated from the politics, and if the environment imposes an entrepreneurial management method indiscriminately on a completely different administrative system, it negatively affects public values such as equity and honesty that the administration has traditionally considered.

Critics' attacks are centered on the fact that if the government continues to be perceived as a mere provider of services, as advocated in the new public management theory, the crucial national task of calling for a collective choice of citizens is likely to be excluded from the role of the government. Therefore, if a policy decision is made that is associated with a group, class, or regional interest, this model can not give a particular answer.

Especially, securing accountability of contract-type system based on the premise of a democratic state is also essential, which can be said to be the most fundamental task surrounding the new public management theory. It is because no efficient government can function as a government unless it fulfills its public responsibility. Thus, the pursuit of excessive corporate government may increase instrumental rationality, but if it is wrong, it may result in undermining the intrinsic rationality.

Finally, decentralization, one of the characteristics of neo-managerialism, causes unintended problems. In other words, the more decentralized by functional sharing, the more likely it is that a so-called paradox of new managerialism will arise, in which political leaders crave more control and strengthen intervention in the centralized direction.

■ The Relevance of Neo-Liberalism Ideology

Another controversy being put on this model from the political-ideological standpoint is the position of neo-liberalism on which the model is based. From the standpoint of new public management theorists, the purpose of government should be limited to the supply of public goods and services. To this end, the government should shift to a competitive and market-oriented structure, and adopt a cost-minimizing and consumer-centric approach as the management approach. Accordingly, neo-liberalists believe that bureaucrats should be competitive by cutting budgets and workforce as the most powerful means to bring about change.

Despite the advocacy of neoliberal political philosophy, however, the opposition is also formidable. The point of criticism is that the rights of particular classes should be reserved and the behavior of authoritarian rule should not be rationalized to strengthen national competitiveness.

The strengthening of competitiveness pursued by neo-liberalism has the meaning of existence only on the premise that the strengthening of competitiveness of enterprises remarkably improves the lives of the people. Strengthening competitiveness pursued by neoliberalism means existence only if the strengthening of competitiveness of the enterprise ultimately improves the life of the people. In this respect, it is necessary to consider whether an unconditional commitment to a competition-oriented market can solve all problems, including political democratization.

Another problem to be considered with the optimistic view of neoliberal ideology is the fact that new public management reform based on this ideology seems to be effective in reality. From the minimum government theory to the current entrepreneurial paradigm, the question of whether the neo-liberal influence in the reform model of the U.S. government has had the intended effect, and whether it should be regarded as ideology suitable for the environment of developing countries from this angle.

The entrepreneurial paradigm based on neo-liberalism could pose serious problems, considering the most considerable gap between rich and poor in the Reagan administration, which was an advocate of neo-liberalism.

■ The Relevance in Culture and Orientation

There is a difference between culture-free and culture-bound positions as to whether management techniques developed in Western Europe, such as the United Kingdom and the United States, can be applied to other cultures.

However, the application of new public management model based on a small government to developing countries has caused many cultural problems. The question is whether the measures presented in the West where individualistic culture has developed can be applied to countries such as developing countries where collectivism culture has developed. In other words, individual performance evaluation is possible and encouraged in individualistic countries, but in collectivist cultures, this is denied, and somewhat the individual in the group is emphasized.

In another sense, entrepreneurial governments assume efficiency as the most critical value. However, if the basic structure of civil society is weak, the government's actions based on the logic of the efficiency are likely to infringe the rights of citizens or violate due process and the principle of democracy is likely to be severely undermined.

After all, the goal pursued by entrepreneurial governments, such as the pursuit of efficiency, the introduction of competition concepts, results-based evaluation, and mission-oriented organization management, is likely to conflict with the basic principles of democracy, such as due process or guarantee of basic rights of the people.

There is a constant debate on the relevance of the orientation or approach to new public management theory, such as the concept of customer or performance, or competitive orientation, or market-oriented incentive systems. The point of criticism is that, without considering the characteristics of government organizations, directly applying techniques that are not verified or suitable for the administrative environment in the expectation that business management techniques would be superior to those of administration, resulting in side effects such as a decrease in morale of civil servants and an exodus of experience in public office.

In this light, Richard Gordon Darman, who served as budget supervisor in the Bush administration, assessed the recent neo-Neoism as nothing more than a temporary movement, stressing that the government should serve for the value of broader values, such as equity, representation, and responsiveness, and that the Constitution is not competition but a category for the public sector.

In conclusion, the problem is the difference between the government and the business. The reform strategy that ignores this differentiation and identifies the business with the government will inevitably have problems. Therefore, it is wrong to assume that the government should only be moderating or entrepreneurial on the assumption that the government can do anything well.

2) The Applicability of New Public Management Theory

The new public management theory is critically negatively evaluated due to the controversy over the political-philosophical background, ideology, cultural environment, orientation, and relevance of the approach style. In the United Kingdom, already the birthplace of neo-managerialism, the problem began to be highlighted in the *Public Administration* in 1994. Since then, the debate has accelerated in the U.S. as well, with the issue featured in the *Public Administration Review* since 1998. Besides, it has been pointed out that the evaluation of the transplantation of new public management models applied to developing countries has failed.

After all, the new public management model, which is composed of ideologies including a series of beliefs and preferences without being neutral, faces criticism that it is only a model that focuses mainly on cost reduction and tax reduction, which are the targets of interest of developed countries, rather than problems such as how to underdeveloped countries including developing countries, and how to cultivate system capabilities

However, despite such criticisms being applied to the new public management theory, the following is the backside of this paradigm spreading to the government reform model. It is a passion for supporting this theory that maybe the expression of a real problem that the government has not solved, and that citizens want to be treated like customers, even though they are owners of the government.

In conclusion, the reason why the new public management theory has spread vigorously over the past 30 years is a disprove that the administration has not responded appropriately to the changes in the administrative environment that made entrepreneurial thinking highlighted.

If the current anti-government atmosphere is given, the new public management theory is likely to spread to the government pursuing a pragmatic line despite its weaknesses and exaggerations. In particular, by improving customer service, some progress can be made in creating an environment for government recognition and problem-solving.

3.2 New Public Service Theory

3.2.1 The Background of New Public Service Theory

As a post-bureaucratic paradigm emerging under the banner of anti-government, anti-bureaucracy, anti-taxation since the late 1970s, new public management theory has faced a severe challenge. The key to the change in the new public management theory lies in the fact that the citizen, as the owner of the government, has been ruled out to improve the efficiency and responsiveness of the government.

The criticism is also that the government has only strengthened the power of bureaucrats as a result of its focus on matters of where bureaucrats should focus on directional control or rowing. So, the new changes in the administrative sphere are that the power that was concentrated only on the bureaucrats without the citizens being excluded due to the influence of the new public management theory should be returned to the citizen who is the owner of the government.

Therefore, the new paradigm is that it should start again from the perspective of citizens, who are the owners of the government, rather than the bureaucrat-centered power allocation perspective on which the new public management theory has focused. Now, the new public service theory has emerged that the administration should delegate authority that was concentrated on the bureaucrats to the owner, the citizen who is the owner, and convert them to serve the citizen who is the owner, and build a citizen-centered public service system.

1) The Historical Background of New Public Service Theory

The new public management theory, which relied on administrative measures such as cost reduction and tax reduction to improve responsiveness and efficiency, did not work very well even within advanced countries, and only caused severe side effects in developing countries.

The new public management theory faces with criticism that it can be new governance to enhance the national capabilities beyond the resurgence of scientific management theory centered on F. W. Taylor. In addition to this, another criticism is that even if the new public management theory has a status as governance, it should attempt an organic approach to spread the results after trying to a limited institution or area to maximize its utility. Nevertheless, attempts at overly comprehensive and radical approaches have resulted in a reduction in a national capacity.

The new public service theory emerged as a response to the new changes that are being imposed on the state, as well as the reaction to the wrong vision and prescription of the new public management theory. In particular, the new changes that are being imposed on the country are as follows.

First, the government has come to a situation where it has to make more critical policy decisions, away from market-oriented discussions such as privatization and government downsizing that have been going on for decades. In the meantime, the government has relied heavily on commercial and nonprofit organizations to deliver goods and services from security issues to welfare reform.

However, since local governments mostly connect with these organizations, the role of local governments has become so vital that they are not comparable to conventional ones. Accordingly, a new division of authority is required between the central and local governments following changes in their roles.

Second, the ability of government and NGOs to provide public services has been restricted due to new changes. As a result, government agencies that have been operating based on functional specialization and process control have suffered from coordination difficulties whenever local-based problems arise.

In other words, a well-functioning budget control process under the traditional bureaucracy is not effective in collecting information from civic groups or motivating them, along with how a hierarchical bureaucracy created under the assumption of the direct delivery of services can cope with the increase in services delivered through various civic groups.

As a result, the two concepts of globalization and devolution, which emerged as new agendas, have profound implications for the functions and roles of the state, as well as the traditional bureaucracy structure, have raised the need to build new governance.

First, the problem of adaptation is to integrate the traditional vertical system with a new horizontal system suitable for the challenge of globalization and devolution.

Second, it is to enhance the government's ability to manage state affairs in a changing environment effectively. The government's service system consists of the assumption that services are delivered directly, making it vulnerable in situations where a contractual-dependent professional group of managers must be developed and compensated. The government's service system is constructed under the assumption that it delivers services directly, so it is vulnerable in situations where it is necessary to develop and compensate for a professional manager group that depends on contracts.

Third, it is necessary to categorize what should be done by the central and local governments as a matter of allocation of roles related to the devolution. The importance of local governments and NGOs participating in policy implementation along with the trend of globalization is increasing. As a result, a new role for the central government has to be established concerning the devolution.

Faced with such changes in globalization and devolution, the new public service theory, as new governance, has focused on enhancing national capabilities. For this purpose, instead of the buyer-supplier model emphasized by the new public management theory, it is necessary to strengthen the responsibility based on the individual and local community based on the pluralistic service supply model. It also calls for the dynamic building of relations between the central government, local governments, and civic groups to enhance their ability to respond to changes.

In conclusion, the new public management theory has focused on excluding society, culture, and value system. Therefore, the new public service theory emphasizes that unlike the New Public Service Management Theory, political contexts, rather than economic perspectives, should play a central role in determining the feasibility or direction of the improvement or change of the system's capabilities, including these factors.

2) The Theoretical Background of New Public Service Theory

The theoretical foundation of the new public service theory is the revival of the context that the new public management theory has excluded. This theory is therefore based on the democratic citizenship theory, community and civil society models, organizational humanism and discourse theory, and post-modernism which occupy an essential area in recent political-social theory,

First, democratic citizenship theory based on the new public service theory starts from the problems of representative democratic politics. As public choice theorists argue, a voting system is in the basis of representative democratic politics. However, the assumption of the public choice, which started with a strategy to maximize the interests of individual citizens, is problematic. Thus, it is now the position that citizens should participate in the governance of the whole from a public interest rather than from private interest, abandoning the shortsighted view of simply maximizing individual interests.

This participation is when democratic citizenship with a sense of belonging to the community, along with possession of a long-term view of public affairs, is required. To this end, it is a time when democratic citizenship with a sense of belonging to the community, along with the possession of a long-term perspective on public affairs, is required.

Second, the concept of a new community and the corresponding civil society model is on the basis of the new public service theory. This concept is an alternative to the atomic society due to excessive diversification, which requires a model of the community as a new model to integrate and synthesize it.

As a new model, communitarianism emphasizes that democracy should be established as an essential decision-making process that affects human life, not a democracy, as a procedure for settling disputes. It also emphasizes that citizens should actively participate in the decision-making process. In this respect, the role of government, especially the local government, should play an essential role in maintaining and forming local communities.

Third, the new public service theory is based on organizational humanism. Organizational humanism criticizes that traditional organizational theory emphasizes the objectification, dehumanization, and control-oriented organization operation of organizational members through top-down hierarchical bureaucracy, but has a limited view on human behavior.

Thus, organizational humanism emphasizes that public services are not of a nature that should be assessed solely by objective efficiency and that the interaction of social equity and responsiveness based on the moral and self-determination of bureaucrats has great significance.

In this respect, the new public service theory emphasizes the social equilibrium and responsiveness of the administration that the new public administration emphasized, and argues that bureaucrats should develop standards and means to measure the impact of public services on social equilibrium and the well-being of citizens.

Fourth, two alternatives tend to replace orthodox administration in the administrative domain. These alternatives are new institutionalism and communitarianism, where Charles J. Fox and Hugh T. Miller presented the discourse theory as a third alternative.

According to C. J. Fox, constitutionalism and communitarianism are both not appropriate because they are only interested in justifying administration. Notably, the case of communitarians is problematic because they are interested in justifying the aspect of citizens themselves rather than the legislature as the owner of sovereignty. Thus, when considering the post-modernism conditions, it is unlikely that such a flow would realize the ideal of community, which requires a discourse theory.

3.2.2 The Content and Characteristics of New Public Service Theory

1) The Concept of New Public Service Theory

The new public service theory is a paradigm that emerged as a counteraction to the new public management trend, which the government has stressed too much efficiency ideology, saying it resembles entrepreneurs.

The new public service theory holds that the government should be operated by the joint participation of bureaucrats and citizens and democratic way to improve the status and value of administrative services. Therefore, bureaucrats must provide public services based on democratic principles. Besides, it emphasizes the importance of realizing democratic ideals such as the public interest, governance processes, and the expansion of democratic citizenship.

To this end, the bureaucrats should recognize the complexity of the times' challenges, respect citizens, and learn new skills necessary for policy development and implementation. Especially as a desirable bureaucratic behavior, bureaucrats should put more weight on listening than speaking, and service rather than coordination.

On the other hand, citizens should actively participate in the governance process and should make joint efforts to define and find public issues in terms of cooperation and reciprocity between bureaucrats and citizens. The vital spirit in administration is that the administration is to promote the public interest and to serve the citizen, and it is more important not how efficiently the administration has been carried out but what contribution it has made to improve the quality of life of the citizens.

In conclusion, the new public service theory is based on the theory of civil democracy based on the communitarian theory and discourse theory that have been developed in social science, pointing out the limitations of the control model that the orthodox representative democracy theory puts forward.

Accordingly, the new public service theory focuses on restoring the rights of citizens who are the owners of the government and restoring the community consciousness based on the democracy and equity that has been emphasized by the discourses based on community-based citizenship and citizen democracy. Thus, the new public service theory is a reflection of the times' trend to build a democratic community centered on civil society.

2) The Composition of New Public Service Theory

The new public service theory has a clear difference from the existing administrative paradigm or new public management theory in terms of the contents pursued. The differences through the contents of the new public service theory are as follows.

■ A View on the Role of Administration

The new public service theory emphasizes that the role of administration should be focused on providing services rather than on direction as the new public management theory claims. For that reason, the primary role of government in the past was to take direction, but the future society is so complex that such a role is not only inappropriate, but also impossible. Accordingly, the new public service theory argues that the role of government and bureaucrats should be changed as well.

A View on Policy

The new public service theory argues that it may not be meaningful to think that the result of the government's decision-making process is a policy. For example, policy and project that present directions in the social and political spheres are a mixture of various public opinion and interests, as well as the result of interactions between various groups and organizations.

The new public service theory also emphasizes that policies may appear in unpredictable ways as a result of complex interactions between groups and interests. That is why the government does not have to take full responsibility for its policies, as it is only one actor who plays an essential role in the process of moving society.

A View on the Role of Bureaucrats

The role of bureaucrats emphasized in the new public service theory is not the mission to control citizens and lead society in a new direction as in the past. Instead, it is to help citizens express their common interests and to meet them accordingly. In other words, the primary role of the administration is not to restrict public behavior through regulations or ordinances, as in the past, or to create rules and incentives.

Instead, it is in setting up the agenda to solve problems faced by the community, bringing relevant parties together to promote solutions and seeking negotiations and mediation. New tools require skills necessary for mediation, negotiation, or conflict resolution, not techniques such as management control to play such a role.

■ A View on Public Interest

A View on Public Interest

The new public service theory emphasizes that the public interest should be viewed as a purpose, not a by-product of administration, given the public interest that the administration should pursue. To set the view of the public interest for administration, the bureaucrats must build a public interest concept that everyone can share. As public choice theorists claim, public interest in the new public service theory is not merely summed up individual interests, but rather the result of conversation and discourse on the value shared.

From this point of view, the new public service theory emphasizes that the process of setting goals or visions that society should pursue should not be given to elected political leaders or appointed bureaucrats, but should be done through broad public discourse and discussion.

Role of Government and Bureaucrats Concerning the Public Interest

The new public service theory emphasizes that the role of the government is to create an atmosphere so that a genuine discourse on the direction of society can be possible, in that only a comprehensive vision of community, government or state will be an ideology that leads the future.

In addition to this facilitative role of the government, the government should also take moral responsibility to ensure that solutions are consistent with the norms of justice and fairness. For example, while the government tries to solve public problems, it also has to take responsibility to ensure that these solutions are consistent with the public interest in terms of both nature and process. The role of the government means that it must come to the point where it must ensure that the solution and formation process of the public interest are consistent with democratic norms such as justice, fairness or equity.

In conclusion, bureaucrats should focus on the role of creating an arena for activities so that citizens can express shared values through discourse and develop them into a collective sense of public interest. The role of bureaucrats is not merely to compromise different arguments, but to enable citizens to understand one another's interests and to accept a long-term and broad sense of community and social interests.

■ A View on Strategic Thinking and Democratic Behavior

Role of Government in Realizing the Vision

Another administrative role that the new public service theory emphasizes is about strategic thinking and democratic behavior. It is necessary to establish roles and responsibilities accordingly and to develop specific steps of action to move towards shared goals for realizing the agreed vision. What is essential in the realization of the vision should not merely leave the responsibility for the execution to the bureaucrats after the creation of the vision, but should involve all parties involved in the process of the project.

The role required by the government in this process is to encourage citizens to participate in programs related to civic education or to cultivate leaders widely to raise citizens' pride and responsibility. Thus, it is expected that citizens' self-esteem and accountability will develop into participation will by creating opportunities for all parties to participate and collaborate for the local community.

Role of Political Leaders in Realizing the Vision

The role required of political leaders to elevate the atmosphere is to strengthen civic responsibility, to nurture the solidarity of local communities, and to support the groups and individuals involved. As such, the government cannot directly create a local community, so the government or political leader has to lay the necessary groundwork for responsible civic action.

However, for the facilitative or supportive role in succeeding, the government must give the recognition that it exists to meet the needs of the citizens. To do so, the government should make citizens aware that it is always open and accessible.

■ A View on Citizens and Government

A View on Citizens

Unlike the new public management theory, the new public service theory is a position to start from serving citizens instead of treating them as customers. So the new public service theory emphasizes that bureaucrats should not just respond to the customer's demands of being customers, but focus on building trust and cooperative relationships with citizens.

In this sense, the new public service theory places great emphasis on the fact that the relationship between the government and citizens is different from that of businesses and customers. That is why the government has to provide more services to citizens than customers directly supplied with the service. The government should provide services to those who do not actively seek services but think they will need them, or even those who are future generations of service recipients and even those who do not want to.

As such, the government should provide services to citizens beyond the legal meaning. However, from the standpoint of the new public service theory, the government needs to provide more services than to improve the quality of public services and provide them to customers. However, it is not suitable for the government to respond exclusively in advance, even if it is selfish or short-term customer interests.

In conclusion, the government's emphasis on the new public service theory should be a reality that responds to the needs and interests of citizens, not the position of customers. The virtues emphasized in the new public service theory demand more people to fulfill their responsibilities as citizens of the local community, and governments also need to be sensitive to the needs of citizens.

Responsibility of Government

The new public service theory calls for more than the profit-seeking, which was emphasized by the new public management theory as the responsibility of the government. The categories of responsibility that the government should carry out are not merely in achieving profit-seeking, but in a wide range of ways, ranging from the Constitution, law, community values, political norms, professional standards, and citizen understanding.

Besides, the nature of the government's responsibilities stipulated in the new public service theory is also very complex. For example, bureaucrats often caught up in value confusion amid conflicting or overlapping norms. The new public service theory says that in such cases, bureaucrats should take the situation as it is and seriously consider how they can and should serve citizens and the public interest.

However, the most critical thing in this situation is that bureaucrats should not make policy decisions on their own. Instead, it emphasizes the importance of bureaucratic negotiating capabilities in terms of the need to resolve the issue through the broad involvement of citizens who have been delegated to dialogue, mediation, or authority.

In the end, it is the role of the bureaucracy to inform citizens of various conflicting variables so that reality becomes part of the discourse process. The new public service theory thinks that this is the only way to make real solutions possible and to build civic spirit and accountability.

■ A View on Human Beings and Values

A View on Human Beings

In the context of the new public service theory, what is emphasized with citizens is a new perspective on human beings. The new public service theory criticizes the perspective of the new public management theory that places more emphasis on productivity than people and recommends giving the highest value and focus on people rather than productivity.

An organization can succeed when it is run through a collaborative process and shared leadership concerning humans. The new public service theory does not deny that factors such as productivity improvement emphasized by the new public management theory or redesign or performance measurement of the work process are essential tools for designing a management system.

Nevertheless, what is vital in the management system is that management through people is more important than anything else. Thus, if the organization does not pay enough attention and attention to the values and interests of individuals, it predicts that reasonable attempts to control human behavior will fail in the long run. In other words, for bureaucrats to treat citizens with respect in government organizations, those who manage government organizations should treat bureaucrats with respect.

As traditional administration emphasizes, bureaucrats do not only want the safety of bureaucracy, but they are not participants in the market, as the new public management do. Bureaucrats want to be distinguished from others in that they value other factors than stable salaries, such as motivation or compensation. In this respect, the concept of shared leadership is vital to provide opportunities for civil servants and citizens to identify and act based on motivation and value for public services

The shared leadership emphasized in the new public service theory focuses on the purpose, values, or ideals pursued by organizations and society, which is characterized by mutual respect, acceptance, and support. Leadership performed with people through people plays an essential role in changing participants and transferring them to higher values.

In the end, the core concept of human beings pursued by the new public service theory is that the productivity-oriented management system can result in the improvement of efficiency. However, it will fail to cultivate bureaucrats and citizens who are faithful to the citizenship and devote themselves to their work responsibly.

A View on the Value

The new public service theory emphasizes that the value of citizenship and public service is a higher concept than an entrepreneurial spirit. The new public service theory argues that bureaucrats should not commit foolishness to reduce their goals as a result of expecting them to think and act like entrepreneurs.

The new public service theory defines the responsibility of bureaucrats as the manager of public funds, as the keeper of public organizations, as the trigger of citizenship and democratic discourse, as a catalyst for community establishment, and as a leader of frontline work, serving the citizens.

Concerning these value issues, the new public service theory provides meaningful implications for the challenges and responsibilities that bureaucrats face.

First, bureaucrats must understand and manage more than the content and resources required by the project. If bureaucrats cannot get away from the narrow viewpoint like the past, it will not help the citizens who are at odds with the understanding of the administrative agency.

It is not always the case, but the problems that citizens face are multifaceted or fluid, so they do not easily match the work area of administrative agencies. Therefore, for bureaucrats to serve the citizens, it is necessary to link local communities to work process of administrative processes.

Second, the risk that the bureaucrats have to bear is different from the risk burden that entrepreneurs have. The risk burden and opportunity of bureaucrats emphasized in the new public service theory exist in the framework of joint responsibility with citizens. So this is an essential factor to consider when the discourse and citizen intervention that the new public service theory pursues is always fulfilled, that is, the opportunity and the potential risk burden is recognized are like this. By that standard, the benefits of the dangerous actions that bureaucrats will take when opportunities come are time to exceed the costs of trust, cooperation, and shared responsibility.

3) The Content Characteristics of New Public Service Theory

The content characteristics of the new public service theory can be divided into three aspects.

■ The Theoretical Characteristics

The new public service theory is based on community theory and discourse based on democratic theory, unlike the traditional administration theory that values authority and control of bureaucrats and the new public management theory that calls for management to be like a business.

The new public service theory is a paradigm that has a characteristic in reviving the spirit of democracy by putting the epistemological basis on various knowledge systems that encompass positivism, hermeneutics, critical theory, and post-modernism. Accordingly, to revive the spirit of democracy, the new public service theory revived the importance of the discourse which was damaged by the new public management theory, especially in the process of forming the public interest. It is also meaningful that it suggested the establishment of citizenship based on the spirit of community as the practice field of discourse.

■ The Characteristics of Government' Role and Citizen's View

The new public service theory emphasizes that the role or responsibility of the government to practice the public interest becomes the subject of service to the citizens, away from the level of whether the bureaucrat should row or present the direction as the claim of the new public management theorist.

The concept of newly revived service implies that this should contribute to creating shared values and mediating and negotiating interests between citizens and local communities, not just direct services for customers who were proclaimed in the new public management theory. The significance of the concept of service as a new role of the government that emerged from the new public service theory is that this concept appropriately reflects the dynamics of society.

■ The Characteristics of Policy and Bureaucrat's View

The new public service theory emphasized that even the top-down executive body, which has played an essential role in achieving policy goals, should now achieve the goals through a coalition among organizations, not by means such as incentive system through individual motivation that has been emphasized in traditional administrative theory or new public management theory.

Especially when it comes to the issue of accountability, the new public service theory emphasizes that the responsibility is infinite

[Table 3] Comparison of New Public Management Theory and New Public Service Theory

Type / Perspective	New Public Management Theory	New Public Service Theory
Foundation of theory and recognition	• Economic theory • Sophisticated discussion-based on positive social science	• Democratic theory • Various approaches including positivism, hermeneutics, critical theory, post-modernism
Rationality model and behavioral model	• Technical and economic rationality • Economists or decision-makers based on self-interest	• Strategic rationality • Multiple verifications of political, economic and organizational rationality
Position on the public interest	• Gross profits of individuals	• Result of discourse on shared values
Bureaucrat's reaction target	• Customers	• Citizen
Role of government	• Direction(Catalyst utilizing market power)	• Service (Negotiating and mediating interests in citizens and local communities, creating shared value)
Mechanism to achieve policy goals	• Create mechanisms and incentives to achieve policy goals by utilizing individuals and nonprofit organizations	• Build a coalition of public, nonprofit, and individuals to meet agreed on needs
Form of approach to responsibility	• Market-oriented-Totaling individual interests create desirable outcomes for citizens or groups of customers	• Multidimensional-Public officials are involved in-laws, community values, political norms, professional standards and citizens' interests
Administrative discretion	• Allow wider discretion to achieve corporate objectives	• Need discretion, but with constraints and responsibilities
Organizational structure	• Decentralized public organization that performs basic controls	• Collaborative structure with shared leadership both internally and externally
Motivation for bureaucrat	• Entrepreneurship • Ideological desire to reduce the size of the government	• Public services • Need to contribute to society

by emphasizing the multifaceted nature of responsibility, whereas the traditional administrative theory that emphasizes hierarchical responsibility in a microscopic sense or the new public management theory that focuses on profit-seeking in a market-oriented way.

The new public service theory emphasized that the organizational structure exercising authority and responsibility should also be a cooperative structure based on the spirit of democracy. Also, the source of motivation for bureaucrats is not merely income or entrepreneurship, but rather the focus on contribution to society by enhancing public services. To summarize the content characteristics highlighted in the new public service theory is the following Table 3.

As mentioned above, the characteristics of the new public service theory belong to the normative model compared to other models. In other words, the new public service theory is a normative model based on democracy in terms of reviving democratic citizenship and public interests that have been neglected by values such as efficiency and productivity that other models have emphasized over the years.

In conclusion, the new public service theory can be meaningful in that it emphasizes that the role of bureaucrats should be aligned with the function of returning the authority concentrated on bureaucrats to citizens and integrating public interest or discourse among citizens.

3.2.3 The Relevance of New Public Service Theory

1) The Critique of New Public Service Theory

The theory of new public service is meaningful in that it suggests the role of administration in a normative manner in the situation where the rapid increase in civic participation, the discussion of the pluralism of the public interest, and the democratic governance are actively discussed.

In particular, the new public service theory pointed out that the duty of bureaucrats and the exercise of civic consciousness as a role to contribute to the realization of long-term democracy is a critical factor in the development of community society. In this sense, the new public service theory is likely to make a meaningful contribution to the realization of participatory and democratic administration.

However, by overemphasizing the normative characteristics and values of the administration that the new administrative service theory intends to pursue, there is a lack of discussion on the reestablishment of bilateral relations for maintaining practical or instrumental values such as professionalism and efficiency required in the administration. This is the main point of criticism being put on the new public service Theory.

At a time when our society is facing an era of knowledge-based society, information society, and infinite competition, the administration is a process of realizing public interests based on the will of the people, while professionalism in realizing public interests more efficiently and effectively using diverse information, civic engagement and multi-directional communication systems is also required.

2) The Applicability of New Public Service Theory

Although the needs of the times made government organizations and thus pursued various values accordingly, other paradigms were not entirely ignored even while a particular paradigm enjoyed its dominant position. While one paradigm enjoys a superior status at a particular time, the other paradigms have played a meaningful role, though not extensive. In a similar vein, the new public management theory has been dominant in the government area since the late 1970s. However, this did not mean that the interest in democratic citizenship or public interest has not been wholely faded and has played a supporting role in its way.

This interest suggests a crucial implication in discussing the relevance of the new public service theory. It means that there is a value that should be set priorities, not as efficiency or productivity as the value to be pursued by the administration. In other words, virtues such as civil spirit and community consciousness, which are democratic values rather than efficiency as administrative values, should be prioritized, and administrative culture or institutions should be set up to harmonize the diversity of society rapidly.

In the absence of shared values that the government should pursue, and the high distrust of the resulting administration, and in the real politics, where goals are forced by unilateral populism or agitationalism centered on political leaders, the new public service theory can help open a new horizon on how citizens, governments and all groups of society should derive common goals or values.

Also, the new public service theory, which emphasizes the co-operative structure of the government to derive shared values and the infinite responsibilities of bureaucrats to enforce it, will be an essential touchstone for the country with the administrative culture to avoid even passive administrative responsibility.

Notably, the new meaning of service in the role of the government is vital in that it calls for setting up a new role in the traditional bureaucratic model that has been power-oriented and unfamiliar with responses to citizens. Although many discussions and contents will be added to the new paradigm in the future, it is necessary to provide democratic public services to citizens based on discourse and public interest based on citizenship by gathering all the capabilities.

References

[Books]

Albrow, Martin(1970). *Bureaucracy.* London: Pall Mall Press.

Appleby, Paul H.(1949). *Policy and Administration.* Alabama: University of Alabama Press.

Argyris, Chris & Donald Shoen(1978). *Organizational Learning.* Reading: Addison-Wesley.

Bardach, Eugene(1977). *The Implementation Game.* Cambridge, Mass.: MIT Press.

Bellone, Carl J.(1980). Introduction: Some Theoretical Perspective, in C. J. Bellone (ed.). *Organization Theory and the New Public Administration.* Boston, Mass.: Allyn and Bacon, Inc.

Bennis, Warren G.(1966). *Changing Organizations.* NY: McGraw-Hill.

Bennis, Warren G. & Philip E. Slater(1968). *The Temporary Society.* NY: Harper & Row.

______(1984). Transformative Power and Leadership, in Thomas J. Sergiovanni & John E. Corbally (ed.). *Leadership and Organizational Culture.* Urbana: University of Illinois Press.

Bertalanffy, Ludwig von(1968). *General Systems Theory: Foundation, Development, Applications.* NY: George Braziller.

Blau, Peter M.(1956). *Bureaucracy in Modern Society.* Chicago: University of Chicago Press.

______(1963). *Dynamics of Bureaucracy.* Chicago: University of Chicago Press.

Blau, Peter M. & W. Richard Scott(1962). *Formal Organizations: A Comparative Approach.* San Francisco: Chandler Publishing Co.

Buchanan, James M.(1984), Politics without Romance: A Sketch of Positive Public Choice Theory and Its Normative Implications, in James M. Buchanan & Robert D. Tollison(ed.), *The Theory of Public Choice—II*, Ann Arbor, MI: The

University of Michigan Press.

Caiden, Gerald E.(1971). *The Dynamics of Public Administration: Guidelines to Current Transformations in Theory and Practice.* Hinsdale, Ill.: Dryden Press.

______(1982). *Public Administration*(2nd ed.). Pacific Palisades, CA: Palisades Publishers.

Common, Richard(1999). The New Public Management and Policy Transfer: The Role of International Organizations, in Martin Minogue, Charles Polidano, & David Hulme(ed.). *Beyond the New Public Management: Changing Ideas and Practices in Governance.* Northampton, MA: Edward Elgar Publishing, Inc.

Cyert, Richard M. & James G. March(1963). *A Behavioral Theory of the Firm.* Englewood Cliffs: Prentice-Hall.

Denhardt, Robert B.(1981). *In the Shadow of Organization.* Lawrence, KS: Regents Press of Kansas.

______(1993). *The Pursuit of Significance.* Pacific Grove, CA: Wadsworth.

Dimock, Marshall E.(1937). *Modern Politics and Administration.* NY: American Book Company.

Downs, Anthony(1957). *An Economic Theory of Democracy.* NY: Harper & Row.

Dror, Yehezkel(1968). *Public Policymaking Re-examined.* Scranton, PA.: Chandler Publishing Company.

Dubnick, Melvin J.(1994). A Coup against King Bureaucracy, in John J. DiIulio, Jr.(ed). *Deregulating the Public Service: Can Government Be Improved?.* Washington. DC: The Brookings Institution.

Dunleavy, P.(1991). *Democracy, Bureaucracy & Public Choice.* Hemel Hempstead: Harvester Wheatsheaf.

Dunsire, Andrew & Christopher Hood(1989). *Cutback Management in Public Bureaucracies.* Cambridge: Cambridge University Press.

Easton, David(1965). *A Framework for Political Analysis.* Englewood Cliffs, NJ: Prentice-Hall, Inc.

______(1971). *The Political System*, 2nd ed. New York: Alfred A. Knopf.

Edwards Ⅲ, George C.(1980), *Implementing Public Policy.* Washington, D.C.: Congressional Quarterly Press.

Esman, Milton J.(1966). The Politics of Development, in John D. Montgomery & William J. Siffin(eds.), *Approaches to Development, Politics, Administration and Change.* NY: McGraw-Hill.

Farmer, David J.(1995). *The Language of Public Administration-Bureaucracy;*

Modernity, and Postmodernity. Tuscaloosa, Alabama: The University of Alabama Press.

Fayol, Henri(1949). *General and Industrial Management*. trans, by Constance Storrs. London: Sir Issac Pitman & Sons.

Feldman, Allan(1980), Welfare Economics and Social Choice Theory, Boston: Martinus Nijhoff Publish.

Ferlie, Ewan, Ashburner Lynn, Fitzgerald Louise, & Pettigrew Andrew(1996). *The Public Management in Action*. Oxford: Oxford University Press.

Fesler, James W.(1975). Public Administration and the Social Sciences: 1946 to 1960, in Frederick C. Mosher(ed.). *American Public Administration: Past, Present, Future*. Alabama: University of Alabama Press.

______(1980). *Public Administration: Theory and Practice*. Englewood Cliffs. NJ: Prentice-Hall, Inc.

Fox, Charles J. & Hugh T. Miller(1995). *Postmodern Public Administration: toward Discourse*. Thousand Oaks, CA: Sage Publications.

Frederickson, H. George(1971). Toward a New Public Administration, in Frank Marini (ed.). *Toward a New Public Administration: The Minnowbrook Perspective*. Scranton: Chandler Publishing Co.

______(1980). *New Public Administration*. Alabama: The University of Alabama Press.

Gant, George(1979). *Development Administration: Concept, Goals, Methods*. Madison, Wisconsin: University of Wisconsin Press.

Giddens, Anthony(1994). *Beyond Left and Right: The Future of Radical Politics*. Oxford: Blackwell Publishers Ltd.

Goodsell, Charles T.(1985). *The Case for Bureaucracy: A Public Administration Ploemic*. Chatham, NJ: Chatham House Publishers.

Gouldner, Alvin W.(1954). *Patterns of Industrial Bureaucracy*. Glencoe, Ill.: The Free Press.

Gulick, Luther & Lyndall Urwick(eds.)(1937). *Papers on Science of Administration*. NY: Institute of Public Administration, Columbia University Press.

Haas, Michael & Theodore L. Becker(1970). The Behavioral Revolution and After, in Michael Haas & Henry S. Kariel(ed.). *Approaches to the Study of Political Science*. Scranton, Penn.: Chandler Publishing Co.

Handerson, A. M. & Talcott Parsons(1947). *The Theory of Social and Economic Organization*. NY: Oxford University Press.

Harmon, Michael M.(1981). *Action Theory for Public Administration*. NY: Longman.

Harmon, Michael & R. T. Mayer(1986). *Organization Theory for Public Administration.* Boston: Little & Brown.

Heady, Ferrel(1962). Comparative Public Administration: Concerns and Priorities, in Ferrel Heady & Sybil L. Srokes(eds.). *Papers in Comparative Public Administration.* Ann Arbor: Institute of Public Administration, University of Michigan.

______(1979). *Public Administration: A Comparative Perspective.* NY: Marcel Dekker, Inc.

Hobbes, Thomas(1950). *Leviathan*, NY: Dutton.

Hood, Christopher(1986). *Administration Analysis.* Hempel Hempstead: Harvester Wheatsheaf.

______(1987). Public Administration, in V. Bogdanor(ed.). *The Blackwell Encyclopedia of Political Institutions.* Oxford: Basil Blackwell.

Kahneman, Daniel & Amos Tversky(2000). *Choices, Values, and Frames.* Cambridge: Cambridge University Press.

Katz, Daniel & Robert L. Kahn(1966). *The Social Psychology of Organization.* NY: Wiley.

Katz, Saul M.(1971). Exploring a System Approach to Development Administration, in Fred W. Riggs(ed.). *Frontiers of Development Administration.* Duke University Press.

Kerlinger, Fred N.(1973). *Foundations of Behavioral Research.* NY: Holt, Rinehart and Winston.

Kettl, Donald F.(1994). Deregulating at the Boundaries of Government: Would It Help?, in John J. DiIulio. Jr.(ed). *Deregulating the Public Service: Can Government Be Improved?.* Washington. DC: The Brookings Institution.

Kettl, Donald F. & Jon J. DiIulio(eds.)(1995). *Inside the Reinvention Machine.* Washington, DC: The Brookings Institution.

Kuhn, Thomas S.(1962). *The Structure of Scientific Revolutio*n. Chicago, Ill: The University of Chicago Press.

Lowi, Theodore J.(1979). *The End of Liberalism.* NY: W. W. Norton and Company.

Lynn, Lawrence E.(1996). *Public Management as Art, Science, and Professio*n. Chatham, NJ: Chatham Houes.

March, James G. & John P. Olsen (1976). *Ambiguity and Choice in Organizations.* Bergen, Norway: Universitietforlaget.

______(1995). *Democratic Governanc*e. NY: The Free Press.

March, James G. & Herbert A. Simon(1958). *Organizations*. NY: John Wiley & Sons.

Marini, Frank(ed.)(1971). *Toward a New Public Administration: The Minnowbrook Perspective*. Scranton: Chandler Publishing Co.

Marx, Frits Moretein(1957). *The Administrative State: An Introduction to Bureaucracy*. Chicago: The University of Chicago Press.

McCurdy, Howard E.(1972). *Public Administration: A Bibliography*. Washington, DC: The American University Press.

McKevit, David(1998). *Managing Core Public Services*. Oxford: Blackwell Publisher.

Merton, Robert K.(ed.)(1952). *Reader in Bureaucracy*. Glencoe, Ill: The Free Press.

Minogue, Martin(1998). Changing the State: Concepts and Practice in the Reform of the Public Sector, in Martin Minogue, Charles Polidano, & David Hulme (ed.)(1999). *Beyond the New Public Management-Changing Ideas and Practices in Governance*. Northampton, MA: Edward Elgar Publishing, Inc.

Minogue, Martin, Charles Polidano, & David Hulme(ed.)(1999). *Beyond the New Public Management: Changing Ideas and Practices in Governance*. Northampton, MA: Edward Elgar Publishing, Inc.

Mooney, James D. & Alan D. Reiley(1931). *Onward Industry*. NY: Harper & Row.

Mosher, William E. & J. Donald Kingsley(1936). *Public Personnel Administration*. NY: Harper & Bros.

Mouzelis, Nicos. P.(1975). *Organization and Bureaucracy*. London: Routledge and Kegan Paul.

Nakamura, Robert T. & Frank Smallwood(1980). *The Politics of Policy Implementation*. NY: St. Martin's Press.

Oakshott, Michael(1960). *Hobbes's Leviathan*. Oxford: Basil Blackwill.

Osborne, David & Ted Gaebler(1992). *Reinventing Government: How the Entreprenurial Spirit is* Transfoming *the Public Sector*. NY: Addison-Wesley.

Osborne, David & Peter Plastrik(1997). *Banishing Bureaucracy*. Reading, MA: Addison-Wesley.

Ostrom, Vincent A.(1973). *The Intellectual Crisis in American Public Administration*. Tuscaloosa: The University of Alabama Press.

Peters, B. Guy(1999). *Institutional Theory in Political Science: The 'New Institutionalism.'* London & New York: Pinter.

Pollitt, Christopher(1993). *Managerialism and the Public Services*. Oxford: Blackwell Publishers Ltd.

Quinn, Robert E.(1988). *Beyond Management: Mastering the Paradoxes and*

Competing Demands of High Performance, San Francisco: Jossey-Bass.

Quinn, Robert E. & Kim S. Cameron(eds.)(1988). *Paradox and Transformation: Toward a Theory of Change in Organization and Management*, Cambridge: Ballinger Publishing Company.

Riggs, Fred W.(1957). Agraria and Industria, in W. J. Siffin(ed.). *Toward the Comparative Study of Public Administration*. Bloomington: Indiana University Press.

______(1964). *Administration in Developing Countries: The Theory of Prismatic Society*. Boston: Houghton Mifflin.

______(1994). Conceptual Homogenization of a Heterogeneous Field: Presidentialism in Comparative Perspective, in Mattei Dogan & Ali Kazancigil(eds.). *Comparing Nations: Concepts, Strategies, Substance*. Oxford: Blackwell.

Rosenbloom, David H.(1994). *The Government Performance and Results Act: Early Implementation, The Context of Management Reforms. Post Symposia Information*. Washington, D.C.: Institute for Effective Public Management, Washington Public Affairs Center.

Sabatier, Paul A. & Hank C. Jenkin-Smith(1993). *Policy Change and Learning: An Advocacy Coalition Approach*. Boulder, CO: Westview Press.

Savas, Emanuel S.(1982). *The Privatizing The Public Sector: How to Shrink Government*. NJ: Chatham House Publishers, Inc.

______(1987). *Privatization: The Key to Better Government*. NJ: Chatham House Publishers, Inc.

Sayre, Wallace S.(1957). *Main Stages in the Development of the Study of Public Administration in the United States*. Special Paper on Seminar. Colombia: Teachers College of Colombia University.

Schiro, James Jr.(1996). *The Paradox Principles-How High Performance Companies Manage Chaos, Complexity, and Contradiction to Achieve Superior Results*. Chicago: Irwin.

Scott, William G.(1981). *Organizations: Rational, Natural, and Open Systems*. NJ: Prentic- Hall.

Self, Peter(1993). *Government by the Market: The Politics of Public Choice*. London: The Macmillan Press.

Selznick, Philip(1949). *TVA and the Grass Roots*. Berkeley: University of California Press.

Shafritz, Jay M. & Albert C. Hyde(1987). *Classics of Public Administration*. Chicago,

Ill: The Dorsey Press.

Simon, Herbert A.(1947). *Administrative Behavior.* NY: Macmillan, Inc.

Simon, Herbert A., Donald W. Smithburg, & Victor A. Thompson(1973). *Public Administration.* Alfred A. Knopf.

Somit, Albert & Joseph Tanenhaus(1967). Political Science as a Learned Discipline: Behavioralism, in Albert Somit & Joseph Tanenhaus. *The Development of American Political Science: From Burges to Behavioralism.* Boston: Allyn and Bacon.

Suchman, Edward(1967). *Evaluative Research.* NY: Russel Sage Foundation.

Sztompka, Piotr(1974). *System and Function Toward a Theory of Society.* NY: Academic Press.

Taylor, Frederick W.(1911). *The Principles of Scientific Management.* NY: Harper & Brothers.

Terry, Larry D.(1995). *Leadership of Public Bureaucracies.* Thousand Oakes, CA: Sage Publications, Inc.

Thaler, Richard H. & Cass R. Sunstein(2008). *Nudge: Improving Decisions about Health, Wealth, and Happiness.* New Haven: Yale University Press.

Thomas, R.(1978). *The British Philosophy of Administration.* London: Longman.

Thompson, Victor A.(1977). Bureaucracy and Bureaupathology, in B. L. Hinton & H. J. Reitz(eds.). *Groups and Organizations: Integrated Readings in the Analysis of Social Behavior.* Belmont, California: Wadsworth Publishing Co.

Turner, Mark(1998). Central-Local Relations in the Asia-Pacific: Convergence or Divergence?, in Martin Minogue, Charles Polidano, & David Hulme (ed.).(1999). *Beyond the New Public Management-Changing Ideas and Practices in Governance.* Northampton, MA: Edward Elgar Publishing, Inc.

Varma, S. P.(1977). *Modern Political Theory.* New Delhi: Vikas Publishing House Pvt Ltd.

Waldo, Dwight(1971). *Public Administration in a Time of Turbulence.* Scranton, PA: Chandler Publishing Co.

______(1980). *The Enterprise of Public Administration.* Novato, CA: Chandler & Sharp Publishers, Inc.

______(1984). *The Administrative State: A Study of the Political Theory of American Public Administration*(2nd ed.). NY: Holmes & Meier Publishers.

Weidner, Edward W.(1962). Development Administration: A New Focus For Research, in Ferrel Heady & Sybil L. Strokes(eds.). *Papers in Comparative Public*

Administration. Ann Arbor: Institute of Public Administration, The University of Michigan.

______(ed.)(1970). *Development Administration in Asia*. Durham, NC: Duke University Press.

Weiss, Carol H.(1972). *Evaluation Research*. Englewood Cliffs, NJ: Prentice-Hall.

White, Leonard D.(1926). *Introduction to the Study of Public Administration*. NY: The Macmillan Co.

Wildavsky, Aaron(1964). *The Politics of the Budgetary Process*. Boston: Little, Brown.

Willoughby, William F.(1927). *Principles of Public Administration*. Baltimore: The Johns Hopkins Press.

______(1929). *Principles of Judicial Administration*. Washington, DC: Brookings Institution.

______(1936). *Principles of Legislative Organization and Administration*. Washington, DC: Brookligns Institution.

Wilson, James Q.(1994). Can the Bureaucracy Be Deregulated? Lessons from Gevernment Agencies, in John DiIulio, Jr.(ed.). *Deregulating the Public Service: Can Government Be Improved?*. Washington, DC: The Brookings Institution.

Wright, Deil S.(1983). *Understanding Intergovernmental Relations*. Pacific Grove, California: Brooks/Cole Publising Co.

Young, Oran R.(1968). *Systems of Political Science*. Englewood Cliffs, NJ: Prentice-Hall.

[Articles]

Balfour, Danny L.(1997). Reforming the Public Service: The Search for a New Tradition. *Public Administration Review*. 57(5).

Boulding, Kenneth E.(1956). General System Theory: The Skeleton of Science. *Management Science*, 2(April).

Cook, Brian J.(1998). Politics, Political Leadership, and Public Management. *Public Administration Review*. 58(3).

Dahl, Robert A.(1947). The Science of Public Administration. *Public Administration Review*. 7(1).

______(1961). The Bahavioral Approach in Political Science: Epitaph for a Monument to a Successful Protest. *American Political Science Review*. 55.

Denhart, Robert B. & Janet Vinzant Denhart(2000). The New Public Service: Serving

Rather than Steering. *Public Administration Review*. 60(6).

Denhardt, Robert B. & Joseph E. Gray(1998). Targeting Community Development in Orange County, Florida. *National Civic Review*. 87(3).

Dimock, Marshall E.(1975). W. G. Willoughby and the Administrative Universal. *Public Administrative Review*. 35.

Dror, Yehezkel(1967). Policy Analysts: A New Professional Role in Government Service. *Public Administration Review*. 27.

Frederickson, H. George(1996). Comparing the Reinventing Government Movement with New Public Administration. *Public Administration Review*. 56(3).

Glaeser, E. L.(2006). Paternalism and Psychology. *The University of Chicago Law Review*. 73.

Goodsell, Charles T.(1992). The Public Administrator as an Artisan. *Public Administrative Review*. 52(3).

Hood, Christopher(1991). A Public Management for All Seasons? *Public Administration*. 69(1).

______(1995). Emerging Issues in Public Administration. *Public Administration*. 73.

Kaboolian, Linda(1998). The New Public Management: Challenging the Boundaries of the Management vs. Administration Debate. *Public Administration Review*. 58(3).

Kettl, Donald F.(2000). The Transformation of Governance: Globalization, Devoltion, and the Role of Government. *Public Administration Review*. 60(6).

March, James G.(1978). Bounded Rationality, Ambiguity, and the Engineering of Choice. *Bell Journal of Economics*. 9.

March, James G. & John P. Olsen (1984). The New Institionalism: Organizational Factors in Political Life. *American Political Science Review*. 78.

Mascarenhas, R. C.(1993). Building an Enterprise Culture in the Public Sector: Reform of the Public Sector in Australia, Britain, and New Zealand. *Public Administration Review*. 53(4).

Merton, Robert K.(1940). Bureaucratic Structure and Personality. *Social Forces*. 19.

Nagel, Jack H.(1997). Radically Reinventing Government: Editor's Introduction. *Journal of Policy Anaysis and Management*. 16(3).

Novick, David(1968). The Origin and History of Program Budgeting. *California Management Review*. 11(1).

Ostrom, Vincent A. & Elinor Ostrom(1971). Public Choice: A Different Approach to the Study of Public Administration. *Public Administration Review*. 13(2).

Page, Richard S.(1969). A New Public Administration? *Public Administration Review.* 29(3).

Perrow, Charles(1973). The Short and Glorious History of Organizational Theory. *Organizational Dynamics.* 2.

Peters, B. Guy & John Pierre(1998). Governance Without Government? Rethinking Public Administration. *Journal of Public Administration Research and Theory.* 8(2).

Riggs, Fred W.(1961). Prismatic Society and Financial Administration. *Administrative Science Quarterly.* 5.

______(1961). Trends in the Comparative Study of Public Administration. Mimeo. *American Society for Public Administration.* 21(2).

Rodgers, Robert & Nanette Rodgers(2000). Defining the Boundaries of Public Administration: Undisciplined Mongrels versus Disciplined Purists. *Public Administration Review.* 60(5).

Schachter, Hindy Lauser(1995). Reinventing Government or Reinventing Ourselves: Two Models for Improving Government Performance. *Public Administration Review.* 55(6).

Schick, Allen(1966). The Road to PPB: The Stages of Budget Reform. *Public Administration Review.* 26(4).

______(1978). The Road from ZBB. *Public Administration Review.* 38(2).

Stillman, Ⅱ. Richard J.(1973). Woodrow Wilson and the Study of Administration: A New Look at an Old Essay. *American Political Science Review.* 67.

Sundquist, James L.(1995). The Concept of Governmental Management: Or What's Missing in the Gore Report. *Public Administration Review.* 55(4).

Svara, James H.(1998). The Politics-Administration Dichotomy Models as Aberration. *Public Administration Review.* 58(1).

Thaler, Richard H. & Cass R. Sunstein(2003). Libertarian Paternalism. *The American Economic Review.* 93(2).

Waldo, Dwight(1952). Development of Theory of Democratic Administration. *American Political Science Review.* 46.

Index

Name

Item

About the Author

Tae Ryong Kim is a professor in the Department of Public Administration at Sangji University. He received his Ph.D. from Seoul National University.

His primary academic interests lie in government reform and administrative theory, including the Korean government and social capital. He has published numerous articles and books. The main books include *New Korean Government*(co-author, 2019), *New Korean Administration*(2017), *Administative Theory*(2017), *Modern Society and NGO*(co-author, 2013), *Social Capital and Volunteerism*(co-author, 2011), *Korean Government Reform: Theory and Practice*(2003), and *New Administration Theory*(co-author, 2003) and *Local Government Reform*(co-author, 2001).

He is the editor-in-chief of *the Korean Society and Public Administration* and past president of the Korean Association for Public Administration and Seoul Association for Public Administration. As a social volunteer, he served as co-president of the Citizens' Coalition for Anti-Corruption Act and as a standing executive chairman of the Citizens' Coalition for Economic Justice. He currently serves as the president of the Academy in the Citizens' Coalition for Economic Justice and a standing executive chairman of the Citizens United for Consumer Sovereignty.

In the government and various organizations, he has served as an advisory committee member of the Prime Minister's Office and the Ministry of Public Administration and Security, as well as the Chairman of the Committee on Employment Advancement and Promotion in the Ministry of the Interior and Safety and as head of the Regulatory Review Committee at the Ministry of Personnel Management.